"Philosopher Stanley Fish onc[e ...] in the same way that Freudian..... is dead. . . . It is everywhere.' Christopher Watkin's remarkable book explains better than any other the nature of Derrida's program and the reasons for its persistence. Watkin corrects misunderstandings and caricatures. Derrida is easy to dismiss when one takes a few of his thoughts out of context. But a great deal of importance must be highlighted. The author engages in a biblical and Reformed critique, one that 'hold[s] fast what is good,' while identifying its evils (1 Thess. 5:21–22). Complete with helpful diagrams, the book is a tour de force. I wish I had possessed it while in graduate school."
  —**William Edgar**, Professor of Apologetics, Westminster
  Theological Seminary

"The Reformed community has long sought to stage a dialogue between Jacques Derrida and Karl Barth, but no one before Christopher Watkin has ever considered initiating a dialogue between Derrida and Barth's Reformed critic Cornelius Van Til. Watkin explains Derrida's fundamental ideas very clearly; more, he shows Calvinists some things that might be gained if they read Derrida with sympathy. Not least of all, the Bible might disclose more of its meaning."
  —**Kevin Hart**, Edwin B. Kyle Professor of Christian
  Studies, University of Virginia

"Chris Watkin has done what I thought was impossible. He has explained Derrida's deconstruction with lucidity, brevity, and charity. Not only that: he has imagined what it would be like for Cornelius Van Til to go toe-to-toe with Derrida in a discussion about language, logic, and the Logos made flesh, all of which figure prominently in John 1:1–18. And if that were not enough, he has done it in just over a hundred pages. Readers who want to know what all the fuss over postmodernity is about would do

well to consult this book. It is an excellent beginning to this new Great Thinkers series."
—**Kevin J. Vanhoozer**, Research Professor of Systematic Theology, Trinity Evangelical Divinity School

Praise for the Great Thinkers Series

"After a long eclipse, intellectual history is back. We are becoming aware, once again, that ideas have consequences. The importance of P&R Publishing's leadership in this trend cannot be overstated. The series Great Thinkers: Critical Studies of Minds That Shape Us is a tool that I wish I had possessed when I was in college and early in my ministry. The scholars examined in this well-chosen group have shaped our minds and habits more than we know. Though succinct, each volume is rich, and displays a balance between what Christians ought to value and what they ought to reject. This is one of the happiest publishing events in a long time."
—**William Edgar**, Professor of Apologetics, Westminster Theological Seminary

"When I was beginning my studies of theology and philosophy during the 1950s and '60s, I profited enormously from P&R's Modern Thinkers Series. Here were relatively short books on important philosophers and theologians such as Nietzsche, Dewey, Van Til, Barth, and Bultmann, by scholars of Reformed conviction such as Clark, Van Riessen, Ridderbos, Polman, and Zuidema. These books did not merely summarize the work of these thinkers; they were serious critical interactions. Today, P&R is resuming and updating the series, now called Great Thinkers. The new books, on people such as Aquinas, Hume, Nietzsche, Derrida, and Foucault, are written by scholars who are experts on these writers. As before, these books are short—around 100 pages. They set forth accurately the views of the thinkers under consideration, and they enter into constructive dialogue, governed by biblical and Reformed convictions. I look forward to the release of all the books being planned and to the good influence they will have on the next generation of philosophers and theologians."

 —**John M. Frame**, Professor of Systematic Theology and Philosophy Emeritus, Reformed Theological Seminary, Orlando

Jacques
DERRIDA

GREAT THINKERS

A Series

Series Editor
Nathan D. Shannon

AVAILABLE IN THE GREAT THINKERS SERIES

Thomas Aquinas, by K. Scott Oliphint
Jacques Derrida, by Christopher Watkin
Karl Marx, by William D. Dennison

FORTHCOMING

Francis Bacon, by David C. Innes
Karl Barth, by Lane G. Tipton
Richard Dawkins, by Ransom H. Poythress
Michel Foucault, by Christopher Watkin
G. W. F. Hegel, by Shao Kai Tseng
David Hume, by James N. Anderson
Friedrich Nietzsche, by Carl R. Trueman
Karl Rahner, by Camden M. Bucey

Jacques
DERRIDA

Christopher Watkin

P&R
PUBLISHING
P.O. BOX 817 • PHILLIPSBURG • NEW JERSEY 08865-0817

ISBN: 978-1-62995-227-7 (pbk)
ISBN: 978-1-62995-228-4 (ePub)
ISBN: 978-1-62995-229-1 (Mobi)

Printed in the United States of America

Library of Congress Cataloging-in-Publication Data

Names: Watkin, Christopher, author.
Title: Jacques Derrida / Christopher Watkin.
Description: Phillipsburg : P&R Publishing, 2017. | Series: Great thinkers | Includes bibliographical references and index.
Identifiers: LCCN 2017016902| ISBN 9781629952277 (pbk.) | ISBN 9781629952284 (epub) | ISBN 9781629952291 (mobi)
Subjects: LCSH: Derrida, Jacques. | Deconstruction. | Van Til, Cornelius, 1895-1987. | Philosophy and religion. | Christian philosophy.
Classification: LCC B2430.D484 W38 2017 | DDC 194--dc23
LC record available at https://lccn.loc.gov/2017016902

To Alison, who waits more graciously,
reads more patiently, and comments more lovingly than I;
and to Benjamin, to add to your bottom shelf.

CONTENTS

SERIES INTRODUCTION

Amid the rise and fall of nations and civilizations, the influence of a few great minds has been profound. Some of these remain relatively obscure even as their thought shapes our world; others have become household names. As we engage our cultural and social contexts as ambassadors and witnesses for Christ, we must identify and test against the Word those thinkers who have so singularly formed the present age.

The Great Thinkers series is designed to meet the need for critically assessing the seminal thoughts of these thinkers. Great Thinkers hosts a colorful roster of authors analyzing primary source material against a background of historical contextual issues, and providing rich theological assessment and response from a Reformed perspective.

Each author was invited to meet a threefold goal, so that each Great Thinkers volume is, first, *academically informed*. The brevity of Great Thinkers volumes sets a premium on each author's command of the subject matter and on the secondary discussions that have shaped each thinker's influence. Our authors identify the most influential features of their thinkers' work and address them with precision and insight. Second, the series maintains a high standard of *biblical and theological faithfulness*. Each volume stands on an epistemic commitment to the "whole counsel of God" (Acts 20:27), and is thereby equipped for fruitful critical engagement. Finally, Great Thinkers texts are *accessible*, not burdened with jargon or unnecessarily difficult vocabulary. The goal is to inform and equip the reader as effectively as possible through clear writing, relevant analysis, and incisive, constructive critique. My hope is that this series will distinguish itself by striking with biblical faithfulness and the riches of Reformed tradition at the central nerves of culture, cultural history, and intellectual heritage.

Bryce Craig, president of P&R Publishing, deserves hearty thanks for his initiative and encouragement in setting the series in motion and seeing it through. Many thanks as well to P&R's director of academic development, John Hughes, who assumed, with cool efficiency, nearly every role on the production side of each volume. The Rev. Mark Moser carried much of the burden in the initial design of the series, acquisitions, and editing of the first several volumes. And the expert participation of Amanda Martin, P&R's editorial director, was essential at every turn. I have long admired P&R Publishing's commitment, steadfast now for over eighty-five years, to publishing excellent books promoting biblical understanding and cultural awareness, especially in the area of Christian apologetics. Sincere thanks to P&R, to these fine brothers and sisters, and to several others not mentioned here for the opportunity to serve as editor of the Great Thinkers series.

Nathan D. Shannon
Seoul, Korea

FOREWORD

If the categorical imperative for civil conversation is "Listen before you speak," the law for philosophical evaluation is "Understand before you critique." More than almost any other major twentieth-century thinker, Jacques Derrida has been abused by critics who ignore both formulations of the ethics of intellectual debate.

For that reason, it seems to me that the first chapter of this book is the most important. It takes the most basic concepts of Derridean deconstruction—such as logocentrism, phonocentrism, "there is nothing outside the text," writing, presence, différance, and metaphysics—and gives accessible and, I believe, accurate accounts of what Derrida was trying to say. Of course, no two Derrida scholars will interpret him in exactly the same way, and there may be quibbles about this or that formulation. But Chris Watkin has set for himself the proper criterion: will those sympathetic to Derrida accept these interpretations? I think he has passed this test with room to spare and has earned the right to proceed to *explicate* the more substantive parts of Derrida's thought (ethics, politics, and theology) and, very importantly, to proceed to *evaluate* his thought as a whole.

Derrida doesn't like to call deconstruction a theory, but I'm afraid he gives us one despite himself. It is a theory about the finitude of language and meaning, its inherent incompleteness and indeterminacy. Derrida presupposes an essentially Hegelian holism. Everything particular is part of a larger whole, and it has its meaning and its being only as part of that whole. It can neither be nor be understood all by itself. "There is no atom" (*Poi*, 137). Thus, to say, "*There is nothing outside of the text*" (*OG*, 158, Derrida's emphasis) is to say that "there is nothing outside of context" (*LI*, 136).

Of course, like so many other post-Hegelian thinkers, Derrida is a holist without the whole. As if meditating on 1 Corinthians 13:9, "For we know [only] in part," he understands our finitude to mean that our meanings always presuppose some total context that we never actually possess, since we are not God. Here is a significant overlap. The atheist author of deconstruction thinks that we are not God. Curiously enough, theistic interpreters of Derrida, such as Watkin and me, are more than a little inclined to agree. It is true that Derrida does not employ the Creator-creature distinction as one between two levels of reality. But he constantly employs the concept of God in some form in order to remind us that we are not absolute, self-grounding, the embodiment of all Goodness, and the thinkers of all Truth.

There is a Kantian/epistemic aspect to Derrida's holism as well as a Hegelian/ontological dimension. The Kantian thesis expresses the fact that Derrida has taken the hermeneutical turn. If it is objected that "being must always already be conceptualized" (*WD*, 74), that is, guided by some *a priori* presuppositions, in order to speak as Derrida does, he grants the point immediately. Deconstruction is an interpretation, but so are the objections and alternatives to it. We live in what Paul Ricoeur calls "the conflict of interpretations," and no one should be more fully aware of this fact than theologians with the slightest knowledge of the history of Christian theology. Our cognition has the form of interpretation, of construal, of seeing something as something, and interpretation is never without presuppositions or perspectives that are vulnerable to revision or replacement.[1] We do not "see" the real directly, but through the lenses of *a priori* assumptions that always embody the limits of our location and often express the biases of our race, gender, class, party, or denomination. Or, to put the latter point theologically, sin often shapes our interpretations in ways that we work hard not to notice (Rom. 1:18).[2] We are not only *finite*; we are *fallen*.

The Hegelian theme is the ontological background for the semantic/epistemic thesis: "*The thing itself is a sign*" (*OG*, 49). It is not just words, sentences, concepts, or theories that point beyond themselves to a larger context on which they are dependent; it is such things as computers, cabbages, and compost piles that, in their being as well as in their meaning, belong to a larger system of reality. By analogy with *ecosystem*, we could speak of their *ontosystems*.

Perhaps you've heard of the homiletics professor who always hammered away on the notion that "a text without a context is a pretext." Derrida's theory of meaning and being, and thus of knowledge and truth, could be expressed in this formula: "Any individual in the world,[3] linguistic or extralinguistic, without its

---

1. Hans-Georg Gadamer speaks of traditions as playing this role, and Michel Foucault gives the part to social practices. On Gadamer, see my analysis in *Whose Interpretation? Which Community? Philosophical Hermeneutics for the Church* (Grand Rapids: Baker Academic, 2009).

2. I have developed this theme in relation to Marx, Nietzsche, and Freud in *Suspicion and Faith: The Religious Uses of Modern Theism* (New York: Fordham University Press, 1998).

3. Emphasis on "in the world." As an atheist, Derrida does not take God to be a real individual.

context is like an emperor without clothes." This suggests that, in spite of Derrida, deconstruction is a kind of method, telling us how to proceed: "Look for the context, uncover the presuppositions, discover what can and cannot be seen from that perspective; in short, find the clothes that fit the emperor and give him whatever human grandeur he deserves, but not more. For we have seen that he is not God."

The term *deconstruction* is often applied to Derrida's substantive ethical, political, and theological views. This can be misleading insofar as it suggests that his deepest convictions about the good and the real are somehow entailed by his semantic and epistemic commitments (as discussed in chapter 1). In my view, this is true only in a very limited, formal sense. Deconstruction as a general theory does place constraints on the metaclaims that we can make about our ethics, our politics, and our theology. Watkin has nicely expressed this at the end of chapter 2:

> Derrida is always against resting on our ethical or political laurels, thinking that we have all the knotty problems solved and all the loose ends tied up and that there is no more hard thinking to do. He is against following established rules and conventions without considering on each occasion whether those rules or conventions are themselves just. He is always against authority setting itself up as unimpeachable or natural, and he incessantly exposes its contingent or artificial origins.

In other words, deconstruction is a warning against treating our meanings as completely clear and our truths as The Truth.

Derrida's most succinct expression of this conclusion is in "Force of Law," where he argues that we should never simply identify the law with justice, or, to put it a bit differently, never identify *our* laws with *The Law*. One could build a rather strong case for such a thesis from the Prophets, Jesus, and Paul. No?

But if deconstructive theory requires us to acknowledge the finitude rather than the finality, the penultimacy rather than the ultimacy, of our theories and practices, I cannot see how it requires the substantive commitments of Derrida in ethics, politics, or religion. It tells us that American Republicans, American Democrats, and even French leftists like himself should be more humble about their ethics and their politics than they usually are. But it does not tell us which, if any, of these traditions we should adopt. All are prejudiced (in the sense of being guided by presuppositions that are not self-evident and are located within perspectives that are not all-seeing) and have come short of godlike, absolute knowing.

This does not require an "anything goes" kind of relativism, according to which all views are equally good (or bad, as Buddhists and the ancient skeptics would say). It seems to me that the situation is something like this:

(1) Our theories and practices are indeed relative to the historically conditioned and particular contexts by which they are supported and that they in turn support.

(2) Christians need not be afraid to acknowledge this. After all, we are relative, and only God is absolute. Biblical revelation does not transubstantiate us from human into divine thinkers and agents. Our understanding of that revelation is always a human interpretation, contested by other interpretations. We try to be open to the Holy Spirit, but unlike thinkers such as Spinoza and Hegel, we do not claim that human thought at its best is the Holy Spirit and that our interpretations are somehow divine.

(3) This does not preclude our thinking that some ethics, politics, or theology is "the best obtainable version of the truth."[4]

4. This is the formula that Woodward and Bernstein developed out of their Watergate experience as the proper goal for journalists. Obviously, if you have a better source, you may well get a better version—but not necessarily. Slavery, Jim Crow, and apartheid all rested in large measure on appeals to Scripture.

Nietzsche, for example, is a radical perspectivist, but he does not think that Christianity or Platonism are just as good as his "will to power" philosophy.

(4) It does mean that the attempt to argue that this version of ethics, politics, or theology is the best available version will be very difficult. The premises and the criteria to which one might appeal are themselves matters in dispute.

(5) We could therefore say that every worldview is a matter of faith. What Ricoeur calls "the conflict of interpretations" is also the conflict of competing faiths—not in the sense of a specifically religious faith, but in the fairly common sense in which we say that beliefs and practices are matters of faith when they cannot be justified by some neutral, objective, universally acknowledged "view from nowhere." Derrida himself says, "I don't know, one has to believe . . ."[5]

In fact, I believe Derrida could (and in effect does) affirm all five of these points, and I see no reason why a Christian should not as well.

I'm suggesting that there are three elements to Derrida's thought: deconstruction as a general theory of meaning, his ethical and political views, and his theology, that is, his atheism. In his mind and in his writings, they are found together, but there is no logical or conceptual connection among them. Each of the three could be consistently held without either of the other two. If this is true, then each needs to be evaluated on its own terms and not condemned as guilty by association with either of the other two dimensions. The unconscionably inaccurate readings that Derrida has too often received seem to stem from the need to discredit the theory of language and meaning in order to

---

5. *Memoirs of the Blind: The Self-Portrait and Other Ruins*, trans. Pascale-Anne Brault and Michael Naas (Chicago: University of Chicago Press, 1993), 129 (Derrida's ellipsis). He links this idea to the difference between believing and seeing (p. 1), as if meditating on John 20:26–29.

protect oneself and one's readers from either the politics or the theology or both. A more careful reading, such as the one that follows, shows that this approach is not only irresponsible but unnecessary.

I have argued elsewhere that Christians can be helped to recapture the critique of religion found in Jesus and the Prophets by reading three famous atheists: Marx, Nietzsche, and Freud.[6] In similar fashion, Christians might benefit from a conversation with Derrida. I have suggested that deconstruction can be read as an extended meditation on the claim that we are not God. Christians, who share this belief with Derrida, might gain important insights by listening to the way in which, through a different lens and from a different location, he makes the point.

The monograph that follows is a fine map for such an exploration.

Merold Westphal
Distinguished Professor of Philosophy Emeritus
Fordham University

6. See note 2 above.

ACKNOWLEDGMENTS

This book came about in a curious way. I am grateful to Charlie Butler and Graham Shearer for indulging me in correspondence on Derrida and then drawing my attention to this series; to Ted Turnau for formal introductions to the folks at P&R; to series editors Nathan Shannon and Mark Moser, and to P&R's director of academic development, John Hughes, for their exemplary encouragement of the project and their help through all its stages; and to those who have read some or all of the manuscript and offered comments along the way, including Bradley Green, Graham and Charlie (again), and Alison. I am very grateful to my father, Kenneth Watkin, for scrupulous and humorous copyediting and for reminding me that only contortionists can fold their hands. I would not have been able to write this at all, had I not been granted gracious indulgence by my wife, Alison; my admiration and love for you are combined with heartfelt thanks. Since becoming a Christian at the age of fifteen and striking out in philosophy at around twenty, I have sought an opportunity to explore Derrida's thought from a biblical point of view. I am grateful that God has now granted me that opportunity and, in the process, has shown me a little more of his vast love (Eph. 3:14–21) and wisdom (Col. 2:1–3).

INTRODUCTION

Although Van Til outlined the terms of a methodology, far more needs to be done with actual arguments, both their form and content. How does one conduct an argument with an adherent of deconstruction?[1]

You must go on, I can't go on. I'll go on.[2]

Why Derrida Matters Today

As I walked down the stairs after lunch, I reflected on what had been one of my more eventful encounters in a Cambridge college dining hall. What I had just experienced seemed to be well summarized by the exclamation of Job, "My ears had heard of you but now my eyes have seen you" (Job 42:5 NIV). My conversation with an elderly gentleman had started predictably

---

1. William Edgar, introduction to *Christian Apologetics*, by Cornelius Van Til (Phillipsburg, NJ: P&R Publishing, 2003), 15.
2. Samuel Beckett, *Three Novels by Samuel Beckett: Molloy, Malone Dies, The Unnamable* (New York: Grove Press, 1958), 414.

enough, with the usual polite opening questions about the state of our respective research, but it was when I made some general comment on a piece I was writing at the time on Derrida that I sensed that the tone of the conversation had changed. The gentleman was still impeccably polite and courteous, but the words that stuck with me from the conversation we conducted over the second half of the meat course and a delicious custard pudding were "intellectual terrorism" and "intention to bring down the whole edifice of rational inquiry and academia." Before we parted, he promised to send me a piece he had written explaining at greater length why Derrida was a dangerous charlatan, and I promised that I would read it. I had of course heard, previous to that encounter, of the infamous "Derrida affair" at Cambridge in 1992, with its indignant letters to the *Times* (London), petitions of fellows, and what, by Cambridge standards, was a veritable popular revolution against the awarding of an honorary degree to the French philosopher Jacques Derrida. I had heard all the stories, but, like the stunned, unsuspecting neighbors of the serial killer interviewed on the nightly news, I never thought that I would experience that sort of thing firsthand.

If I had told my antipathetic lunch partner that one day I would write a book on Derrida and Christianity, I fear we might never have reached the end of the delicious tart and custard. If the views of the readers of this book are even half as polarized as some of the opinions I encountered as a graduate student (I remember one exasperated lecturer insisting in a graduate seminar on Derrida that "of course he's a real philosopher, for G*d's sake"), then I certainly have my work cut out. To write on one controversial subject may be regarded as misfortune; to write on two at the same time looks like foolhardiness, for most readers who are sympathetic to Derrida will probably not like Reformed Christianity, and most Reformed Christian readers will probably not like Derrida.

I write this book neither to praise Derrida nor to bury him. The evangelical and Reformed reception of Derrida has too often followed Mark Antony's verdict on the dead Caesar: "The evil that men do lives after them; the good is oft interred with their bones." I hope that my book has avoided this rather ungracious approach to eulogy. Nevertheless, given the controversy that still surrounds Derrida's thought, a word of justification is required for his inclusion in a series of volumes on "Great Thinkers."

Derrida was the author or coauthor of at least seventy books, held professorships in Paris and the University of California, Irvine, and received honorary doctorates at many more universities (including Cambridge: the petition failed in the end), but that says very little about the scope of his influence. It is only slightly more illuminating to point out that there are now at least eighty-six book-length studies with "Derrida and . . ." in the title, including *Derrida and Antiquity, Derrida and Autobiography, Derrida and the Writing of the Body, Derrida and the Future of Literature, Derrida and Religion, Jacques Derrida and the Humanities, Derrida and Legal Philosophy, Derrida and Feminism, Derrida and Queer Theory,* and *Derrida and Democracy.* According to Derrida's friend and collaborator Geoffrey Bennington, his work has been translated into a dozen languages.[3] The dust jacket of Christopher Norris's *Derrida* describes him as "undoubtedly the single most influential figure in current Anglo-American literary theory."[4] Writing in the *New York Times* in 1998, Dinitia Smith referred to Derrida as "perhaps the world's most famous philosopher—if not the only famous philosopher."[5] Leslie Hill, one of Derrida's most astute and sure-footed commentators, describes his writing

---

3. Geoffrey Bennington and Jacques Derrida, *Jacques Derrida,* trans. Geoffrey Bennington (Chicago: University of Chicago Press, 1993), 358.

4. Christopher Norris, *Derrida* (Cambridge, MA: Harvard University Press, 1987).

5. Dinitia Smith, "Philosopher Gamely in Defense of his Ideas," *New York Times,*

as simply "one of the essential events in the history of modern thought,"[6] part of "a remarkably creative generation who collectively, within twenty years or so, radically changed the whole philosophical and theoretical landscape both in France and elsewhere."[7] Nevertheless, piling up quotations like this will neither convince the skeptical nor inform the interested, and neither of these constituencies, I suspect, would wish me to waste any more time before getting down to discussing Derrida in detail.

The Structure and Approach of This Book

The first half of this book will seek to set out, as succinctly and clearly as possible, some of the most important aspects of Derrida's writing on metaphysics, ethics/politics, and theology. This first part will necessarily be schematic and reductive, and any readers who find that unacceptable are welcome to begin reading Derrida in the original French for themselves, for any translation, interpretation, or summary of any length is to some extent a betrayal of complexity. What I offer can be thought of as a map of some important aspects of Derrida's thinking. Every map greatly simplifies the territory it represents, but every map is also useful in some situations and for some ends. The map of the London Tube system is a derisory representation of relative geographical locations, but it serves very well the purpose of helping people navigate from station to station. Providing we do not confuse it with the territory it describes, it is very helpful indeed.

The second half of the book will seek to evaluate Derrida's

May 30, 1998, http://www.nytimes.com/1998/05/30/arts/philosopher-gamely-in
-defense-of-his-ideas.html (accessed January 7, 2016).

6. Leslie Hill, *The Cambridge Introduction to Jacques Derrida* (Cambridge: Cambridge University Press, 2007), viii.

7. Ibid., 3.

thought in these three areas from the viewpoint of a Reformed, and specifically Van Tilian, position. My aim is neither to dash off a Reformed "takedown" of Derrida nor simply to suggest that he is much closer to Reformed Christianity than many have thought. My intention is to evaluate Derrida's positions in the light of biblical doctrines that, I will argue, most often take him by surprise and cut across both the objects of his critique and his own ideas. It avails us little to criticize Derrida for not being a Reformed theologian, or, for that matter, to criticize Reformed theology for not being deconstruction. To do so would be like critiquing a baseball player for not scoring touchdowns, or accusing a square of not being circular. Derrida is not a failed Reformed theologian, and Reformed theology is not deficient deconstruction. It is therefore my intention to let both deconstruction and Reformed theology speak in their own terms, bringing with them their own assumptions, and to seek to draw distinctions and comparisons between the two in a way that is, as far as possible, fair to what both Derrida and the Bible actually say. My aim is to provide Christians with a way of understanding Derrida that does justice both to his own thinking in its own terms, and to the Bible in its.

Although I hope my analyses and interpretations will stand for themselves, I perhaps owe the reader at the outset some explanation of my methodology. First, I write as a Christian for a Christian publishing house. Second, I start with the assumption that one must earn the right to critique a position by understanding it and being able to express it in a way that its adherents will be happy to own and endorse as correct. It is the important principle of *audi alteram partem*: listen to the other side. In terms of understanding a philosopher's writing, this means that until we have understood not only what position someone holds, but also the reasons why he holds it—or, in other words, why that person finds his position attractive—we have not yet understood it. If it makes no sense to us why Derrida would say something or why, looking at the world through his eyes, it would be an important or good thing to say, we need to keep reading and thinking some more before we open our mouths or pick up our pens to pass comment on him. I ask Christian readers not to leap into criticisms of Derrida's positions before they have walked a mile in his shoes and before they have understood why those positions are appealing and attractive to him. Likewise, I ask readers of this book who are sympathetic to Derrida, but hostile to a Reformed Christian position, to extend the reciprocal courtesy. Some readers may become a little frustrated that I do not get down to critiquing Derrida until the second half of the book. As it happens, this is a constraint of the Great Thinkers series, but I embrace it enthusiastically because it allows us to obtain a clear idea of what Derrida is saying in his own terms before we begin discussing how it relates to Reformed Christianity.

After *audi alteram partem*, my second guiding principle is that, within the created order, there is nothing that is completely and exhaustively good, nor anything that is utterly and unremittingly evil. Only God is good (Luke 18:19), and even the worst aspects of his originally good but fallen creation retain a dim flicker of goodness. This gives the Christian a particular predisposition, not only toward Derrida, but toward all aspects of every culture: we expect to find both good and bad there. It gives the Christian cultural critic, I would suggest, an unusual openness and curiosity.[8]

Finally, some of the secondary literature on deconstruction seems to assume that in order to write well on Derrida we must

---

8. This point is made by Tim Keller in the series of lectures *Preaching Christ in a Postmodern World*, available at https://itunes.apple.com/au/itunes-u/preaching -christ-in-postmodern/id378879885?mt=10# (accessed January 16, 2016).

write like Derrida. This is silly. It is just as silly as saying that, in order to write well about Shakespeare, we have to pepper our prose with the occasional *prithee* and *forsooth* and compose our thoughts in blank verse. Derrida's style has caused much frustration and controversy among some of his readers, and he has his reasons for writing as he does, some of which I shall seek to explain below. In order to show what those reasons are, however, or in order to explain his thought more generally, trying to imitate his idiom would prove to be more of a hindrance than a help.

ABBREVIATIONS

Works by Derrida

AL	*Acts of Literature*
AR	*Acts of Religion*
C	"Circumfession"
DCP	*Debates in Continental Philosophy: Dialogues with Contemporary Thinkers*
DI	"Declarations of Independence"
DN	*Deconstruction in a Nutshell*
FL	"Force of Law"
FT	"Following Theory"
FWT	*For What Tomorrow—A Dialogue*
GD	*The Gift of Death*
GT	*Given Time: I. Counterfeit Money*
HJR	"Hospitality, Justice and Responsibility"
LI	*Limited Inc*
LJF	"Letter to a Japanese Friend"
MP	*Margins of Philosophy*
MPdM	*Mémoires: For Paul de Man*
MS	"Marx and Sons"

OG	*Of Grammatology*
OTN	*On the Name*
PF	*Politics of Friendship*
PG	*The Problem of Genesis in Husserl's Philosophy*
Poi	*Points . . . : Interviews, 1974–1994*
Pos	*Positions*
R	*Rogues: Two Essays on Reason*
S	*Signéponge/Signsponge*
SP	*Speech and Phenomena*
TOJ	*"The Time Is Out of Joint"*
TS	*A Taste for the Secret*
TSI	*"This Strange Institution Called Literature"*
TTP	*"The Time of a Thesis: Punctuations"*
WD	*Writing and Difference*

Other Works

AGG	John Frame, *Apologetics to the Glory of God*
CTE	Cornelius Van Til, *Christian Theistic Ethics*
CVT	John Frame, *Cornelius Van Til: An Analysis of His Thought*
DCL	John Frame, *The Doctrine of the Christian Life*
DF	Cornelius Van Til, *The Defense of the Faith* (4th ed.)
DG	John Frame, *The Doctrine of God*
DKG	John Frame, *The Doctrine of the Knowledge of God*
HWPT	John Frame, *A History of Western Philosophy and Theology*
ICG	Cornelius Van Til, *The Intellectual Challenge of the Gospel*
IST	Cornelius Van Til, *Introduction to Systematic Theology*

PART 1

DERRIDA'S THOUGHT

The danger of starting the discussion of a philosopher's thought with biographical detail is that it becomes a quick and easy lens through which the work is read and explained. None of us would be content to have everything we say reduced to our biography along the lines of "You are only saying that because, when you were six, such and such happened to you." In an interview, Derrida shows his discomfort with this sort of biographical tyranny:

> Ah, you want me to say things like "I-was-born-in-El Biar-on-the-outskirts-of-Algiers-in-a-petit-bourgeois-family-of-assimilated-Jews-but . . ." Is that really necessary? I can't do it. You will have to help me. (*Poi*, 119–20)

However, it would also be a mistake to swing to the opposite extreme and think that Derrida's books just fell from the sky and had no personal, historical, and social context. So a few words of biographical introduction will, I hope, help to situate some of the discussion that follows.

Jackie Élie Derrida, named after child silent-movie star Jackie Coogan,[1] was born on July 15, 1930, in the city of El Biar in Algeria, which was officially part of France at the time.[2] During the Nazi-sympathizing French Vichy regime of 1940–44, although the young Derrida was top of his class, he was forbidden, as a Jew, from enjoying the privilege of raising the French flag, an honor usually given to the star pupil. In 1942 he ran afoul of the anti-Jewish quotas imposed in Algerian schools and was expelled. Derrida's later description of himself at the time as "a little black and very Arab Jew" (C, 58) highlights his marginality in European society at the time. By the time of the 1968 student riots, when universities were occupied, barricades were built in the streets of Paris, and then-President de Gaulle was brought to the brink of resignation, Derrida was teaching at the prestigious École Normale Supérieure, Rue d'Ulm, and he took an active, though marginal and at times uneasy, role in the demonstrations, marches, committees, and communes of "May '68," admitting later that he was no *soixante-huitard* ("sixty-eighter").[3] Although his academic reputation grew with the publication of three seminal texts in 1967, "as far as dominant Catholic metropolitan French culture was concerned, Derrida was an outsider several times over,"[4] and his renown grew among English-speaking scholars more rapidly than it did in his native France, a trend that continues to this day.

1. Benoît Peeters, *Derrida: A Biography*, trans. Andrew Brown (Cambridge: Polity Press, 2012), 13.

2. After 1848, Algeria was no longer a French colony, as many biographies of Derrida mistakenly suggest, but was officially divided into three *départements* (administrative districts) under the oversight of the French Interior Ministry.

3. Peeters, *Derrida*, 197.

4. Leslie Hill, *The Cambridge Introduction to Jacques Derrida* (Cambridge: Cambridge University Press, 2007), 6.

1

WHAT IS DECONSTRUCTION?

Not Meaninglessness but Openness

During my undergraduate days, I used to have my hair cut at Carmelo, a friendly barbershop on Jesus Lane in Cambridge. It was one of those old-style barbers that still sport the red-and-white-striped pole over the door. One morning, walking down Jesus Lane on my way to lectures, I saw that some scaffolding had been erected overnight outside Carmelo, so that work could be carried out on the structure of the building. The scaffolding, as it happened, was covered with a plastic sheath with those same diagonal red and white stripes, presumably so that absentminded students would be saved from bumping into the steel poles when they returned to college in the early hours of the morning. So now there were two sets of diagonal, red and white stripes side by side. One set of stripes meant something like "come in here and have your hair cut," and the other meant "watch out, don't bang into this." There was nothing so unusual in that.

In the to-and-fro of daily life, we do not find these different meanings for the same red and white stripes particularly

confusing. We do not see laborers taking their tools into the near-
est barbers expecting to do a day's work, and we do not see people
lining up at worksites for a short back and sides. We understand
the meaning of the red and white stripes in terms of the context
in which we meet them. In fact, if we come to think of it, there
is nothing to stop diagonal red and white stripes from taking on
a further and completely unrelated meaning in the future, and
nothing to stop this new meaning from becoming the primary
sense that most people associate with the stripes. The logo for
a new and dominant multinational corporation, perhaps, or
the signature design of a particular fashion label, may become the
primary association for those same stripes. In a similar way,
the rainbow flag over the past decades has become associated,
in the minds of most people, with the gay pride movement.

We can say, therefore, that the meaning of diagonal red
and white stripes is open: in the future, those stripes could,
in theory at least, mean any number of things of which today
we have no inkling. This does not mean the diagonal red and
white stripes are meaningless. Far from it; they have a set of
contextual meanings that is open and in principle infinitely
expandable in the future. We know what they mean now, but
we don't know how those meanings will change or what new
meanings will overshadow them in the future. Finally, if someone were to insist that we tell them what red and white stripes
mean by themselves, outside of any context, we would have to
reply that the question is misguided. Diagonal red and white
stripes do not mean anything "in themselves"; their meaning
only becomes clear within, and is determined by, a particular
context, and contexts change.

This little example helps us understand the misguided nature
of one of the persistent myths peddled about Derrida: that he
thinks language is meaningless. Language, for Derrida, is not
meaningless; its meanings are open in the sense that we cannot

today close down the meaning of any word or sign, such that we have exhaustively explored its context and can be utterly confident it can't possibly mean anything but what we think it means, nor can we be sure it will not accrue new primary meanings in the future. There is no way to preserve meanings in aspic, no way to short-circuit context and petrify particular meanings, preserving them from the shifting sands of time. Furthermore, context is functionally infinite: the context of an utterance can never be completely exhausted. Where do I draw the line in determining, for example, the relevant context of Shakespeare's *Hamlet*? And even if I can answer that question to my own satisfaction, I can never be sure that some new piece of contextual information will not arise that radically alters the way in which we understand the play. For these two reasons, context is always open.

Logocentrism and Phonocentrism

Despite the necessity and unmasterability of context, the Western tradition has almost always tended to act as if context were not open in this way and as if meanings and concepts could be completely and exhaustively present in the words that signify them, as if diagonal red and white stripes meant something in themselves. It is this delusion that Derrida calls "logocentrism"—a way of thinking about things that would "support the determination of the being of the entity as presence" (*OG*, 12). In other words, it imagines that what something is (red and white stripes, dogs, cats, human beings, or the meaning of the words in a sentence) is completely present in the thing itself, not dependent on anything outside of it. To think logocentrically is to affirm that there can be pure being in little atomized parcels and pure meaning outside any context whatever. When he critiques logocentrism, Derrida has in mind something like the Forms or Ideas of Plato, perfect and unblemished realities that exist apart from this world in a "heavenly place" (Greek: *topos ouranios*) outside all particular contexts, and of which everything in this world is an imperfect and shadowy copy.

Allied to this logocentric illusion that meaning can be free of all context, Derrida discerns another prejudice in the Western tradition, one that sees spoken language as immediate and authentic, and written language as distant and second-best. This is phonocentrism, an "absolute proximity of voice and being, of voice and the meaning of being, of voice and the ideality of meaning" (*OG*, 12). In other words, phonocentrism considers meaning to be fully present in spoken language in a way that it is not present in writing. Spoken language is considered immediate because it comes straight out of the body with no mediating technology such as pencil, paper, written linguistic signs, or a computer keyboard. We think of speech as original and writing as secondary, as written-down speech. One of Derrida's major references for this idea is Jean-Jacques Rousseau, who, in a short, little-known, posthumously published piece entitled "Pronunciation," insists that "writing serves only as a supplement to speech" and that "the art of writing is nothing but a mediated representation of thought" (cited in *OG*, 144). What is more, writing for Rousseau is a "dangerous supplement" because it puts a distance between the author and his or her meaning.

"There Is Nothing Outside the Text"

With logocentrism and phonocentrism under our belt, let's dive in now to our first passage from Derrida's writing, which contains perhaps the most famous one-liner in all his work. It shows us how he tries to correct the illusions of logocentrism and phonocentrism: "There is nothing outside the text." It is a statement that is frequently misunderstood, and so it is worth spending some time unpacking it. For those unfamiliar with Derrida's writing, the passage may seem rather daunting, but we will take it slowly, and I will explain it bit by bit:

> If reading must not be content with doubling the text, it cannot legitimately transgress the text toward something other than it, toward a referent (a reality that is metaphysical, historical, psychobiographical, etc.) or toward a signified outside the text whose content could take place, could have taken place outside of language, that is to say, in the sense that we give here to that word, outside of writing in general. That is why the methodological considerations that we risk applying here to an example are closely dependent on general propositions that we have elaborated above; as regards the absence of the referent or the transcendental signified. There is nothing outside of the text. (*OG*, 158)

Let's start with the final sentence and work backwards. In French, it reads "il n'y a pas de hors-texte" (literalistically: "there is no outside-text"). We should notice four things about the phrase:

1. It is a play on "hors-texte," which, as well as meaning (without the hyphen) "outside the text," is a noun in its own right. An *hors-texte* is a frontispiece or a book plate, a piece (usually a reproduction of a painting, a photograph, an engraving, or a facsimile) inserted right at the beginning of a book, which serves to illustrate or explain the book's main subject, guiding our reading of it by pointing to one of its salient moments or showing us something that the author (or perhaps the publisher) wants to draw our attention to.[5] Coming outside the text proper, it has

---

5. It is not, as James K. A. Smith suggests, "the buffer of blank pages at the beginning and the end of a book, the sheets that are without text." See James K. A. Smith,

a certain authority or objectivity that the text itself cannot have in relation to itself (in rather the same way that
the testimony of an "independent" witness carries more
weight in a court of law than the testimony of the accused).
The *hors-texte* comes bound together with the book, but is
not part of the book proper, coming as it does before the
contents page. So one thing Derrida is saying in this little
phrase is that the circulation of meanings in which we find
ourselves has no cheat sheet; nothing stands outside and
over above the meanings that circulate in and around us
to give us a hint of what the "real meaning of it all" is.

2. Such a cheat sheet, or authoritative guide to meaning, is
what Derrida calls in this passage a "transcendental signified." Derrida is taking the term "signified" from the early
twentieth-century Swiss linguist Ferdinand de Saussure
and his important distinction between "signifier" and "signified." For Saussure, a signifier is a sound-image, a series of
sounds that, to take Saussure's own example, form the word
"tree" in a particular language. A signified is the concept
that corresponds to that sound-image, i.e., the idea of a tree.
A transcendental signified would be a concept that does
not defer its meaning to any other signifieds, but stands,
as Derrida says in this passage, "outside of language" in
pure self-sufficiency and isolation. As opposed to all other
signifieds that in turn become signifiers to define other
signifieds, the transcendental signified is necessary "for the
difference between signifier and signified to be somewhere
absolute and irreducible" (*OG*, 20). "Transcendental"
means that it provides the condition of possibility for
meaning in general, because without at least one thing the

Jacques Derrida: Live Theory (New York: Continuum, 2005), 44.

meaning of which is outside language and utterly fixed (for example: God), meanings are not anchored to anything stable. Derrida says that "the sign and divinity have the same place and time of birth" (*OG*, 14), because the way in which the West has traditionally thought about meaning requires God as its condition of possibility.

3. "Text" in this phrase does not just mean "words written down in a book," as if Derrida were saying that "words are the only things that exist." "What I call 'text'," he insists, "implies all the structures called 'real,' 'economic,' 'historical,' socio-institutional, in short: all possible referents" (*LI*, 148). It is a web of meanings that includes, but is not limited to, the meanings of words on a page. Notice also that when Derrida mentions "writing" in our passage, he specifies "in the sense that we give here to that word" and talks about "writing in general." This "writing in general" is what he elsewhere calls "arche-writing," and the next section of this chapter will be given over to explaining in some detail what it means. For now, let us be content to understand it as describing all meaning, whether in written texts or in our lives more broadly: meanings are always differential (defined in terms of what they are not) and deferred (calling upon other meanings in their own definitions). So rather than saying that Derrida means "there is nothing outside language," it is closer to the mark (but not sufficient) to say "there is nothing outside of context" (*LI*, 136). On a number of occasions, Derrida expresses exasperation with those who persist in interpreting him to be claiming that there is nothing outside language:

> I never cease to be surprised by critics who see my work as a declaration that there is nothing beyond language,

that we are imprisoned in language; it is, in fact, saying the exact opposite. The critique of logocentrism is above all else the search for the 'other' and the 'other of language.' (*DCP*, 154)

Just what that "other" is, we shall find out in the section on ethics below.

4. Finally, we need to note the particular philosophical baggage carried by the innocuous-looking words "there is" (in French, *il y a*). Within the tradition in which Derrida is working, "il y a" is the translation of "es gibt" in Heidegger's German, and when Heidegger says "there is" he means something more than you or I intend by those words in casual, everyday conversation. For Heidegger, the world offers itself or is given to our consciousness ("es gibt" is from the verb *geben*, "to give"). Take the example of the cup of coffee on the desk in front of me. It is a collection of atoms, but when I see it, I can't help experiencing it *as* a cup of coffee, with all the cultural connotations that brings with it for human beings (drinkable, warm, stimulant, etc.). Or take the high-pitched noise outside. I can't help experiencing it *as* an ambulance siren, again with all the cultural baggage and associations that brings for an early twenty-first-century Westerner. This "as-structure of being" is pointing out that our concepts and meanings make sense of the world for us: I do not see confusing shapes, but cups of coffee; I do not hear disorienting sounds, but sirens, bells, and whistles. Reality is "given" to my consciousness, already packaged *as* familiar concepts. So the "there is" of "there is nothing outside the text" could be glossed as "Nothing is present to my consciousness as what it is outside the text," and to expand both "there is" and "text" at

once: "Nothing is present to my consciousness as what it is in a way that is outside the differential play of meanings."

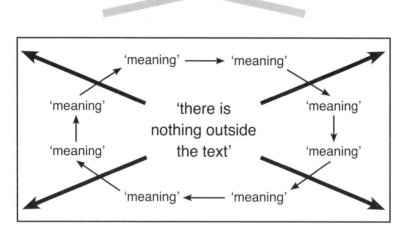

Fig. 1.1. There Is Nothing Outside the Text

The importance of this idea of generalized text, for Derrida, is that rather than there being a Platonic "heavenly place" where the buck stops for meaning, every signified becomes in turn a signifier defining the meaning of other signifieds, and the merry-go-round never stops.

Différance

I suggested above that "there is nothing outside the text" is a necessary way of thinking about meaning for Derrida if we are to avoid what he identifies as the myth of logocentrism. Derrida seeks to expose the myth of phonocentrism (the idea that meaning is fully present in spoken language in a way it is not in writing) by showing that all meaning, not just the meaning of written texts, is never completely present to itself. He has a number of different terms for this condition of non-self-presence, each term with a different slant on the idea. I will try to explain it here in terms of "différance," a French term coined by Derrida. We must understand it if we are to grasp his deconstruction of metaphysics.

First, let us consider what the metaphysics is that Derrida is deconstructing. Western metaphysics, he argues, is distinguished by two main tendencies. First, it is structured in terms of a series of binary oppositions. In each case, one of the two terms in the opposition is privileged over the other: presence/absence, natural/artificial, literal/metaphorical, original/copy, inside/outside, real/imaginary, soul/body, identity/difference, man/woman, human/animal, heterosexuality/other sexualities. Derrida does not have a problem, on an everyday level, with the idea of oppositions as such, nor with the idea that we can make distinctions between things (he is quite happy to do so himself). He has two problems, however, with binary oppositions like those listed above. The first one is that things are not only distinguished, but also hierarchized, with one of them being privileged above the other. This hierarchy leads to exploitation and oppression, as we shall see in the section on ethics below. The second problem is that the oppositions rely on an ideal of purity according to which the privileged element of each opposition can exist by itself, that its meaning can be fully present without needing to refer to the underprivileged element, which deconstruction seeks to point out is simply not the case. What sense is there in "the natural," for example, if there is no "artificial"? Or how can there be an "inside" if there is no "outside"? In each case, the privileged term does not exist in splendid isolation, but relies on the underprivileged term to make it what it is.

The second tendency that characterizes Western metaphysics for Derrida is that it is a "metaphysics of presence." The "presence" referred to here is the idea that (1) the meaning of a signified is fully present in its signifier, rather than being deferred or scattered among plural signifiers, and (2) the meaning of signs is fully and exhaustively present to what Derrida calls an "absolute logos," one who knows perfectly, whom Derrida identifies as God (*OG*, 13). In other words, the West has taken as its blueprint for human knowledge the perfect and immediate knowledge of God, and so "the age of the sign is essentially theological" (*OG*, 14). We can see here echoes of Nietzsche, who affirms that "I am afraid that we have not got rid of God because we still have faith in grammar."[6] We think that our language gives us direct and unmediated access to the world, that it makes the essence of things present to us, but for Nietzsche it does no such thing; it gives us access only to our own human concepts and to the figures of speech inherent in language itself:

> The "thing in itself" (for that is what pure truth, without consequences, would be) is quite incomprehensible to the creators of language and not at all worth aiming for. One designates only the relations of things to man, and to express them one calls on the boldest metaphors. . . . What, then, is truth? A mobile army of metaphors, metonyms, and anthropomorphisms—in short, a sum of human relations which have been enhanced, transposed, and embellished poetically and rhetorically, and which after long use seem firm, canonical, and obligatory to a people: truths are illusions about which one has forgotten that this is what they are; metaphors which are worn out and without sensuous power; coins which have lost

6. Friedrich Nietzsche, *The Anti-Christ, Ecce Homo, Twilight of the Idols and Other Writings*, ed. Aaron Ridley and Judith Norman, trans. Judith Norman (Cambridge: Cambridge University Press, 2005), 170.

their pictures and now matter only as metal, no longer as coins.[7]

Derrida uses a similar image of coins ground down to a smooth surface in his discussion of Anatole France in *Margins of Philosophy*, where he concurs with Nietzsche that "philosophy would be this process of metaphorization which gets carried away" (*MP*, 211).

In his seminal work *Of Grammatology*, Derrida wants to show, therefore, that meaning is not what we think it is: "To make enigmatic what one thinks one understands by the words 'proximity,' 'immediacy,' 'presence' . . . is my final intention in this book" (*OG*, 70). In order to understand how he goes about doing this, let's take again the example of speech and writing and consider Derrida's deconstruction of it with the aid of a series of diagrams. We begin with the traditional Western understanding, according to which the meaning of speech is immediate and present, and writing is distant and imperfect. We can represent this idea by speech being to the left of writing (i.e., before it) and above writing (i.e., privileged over it).

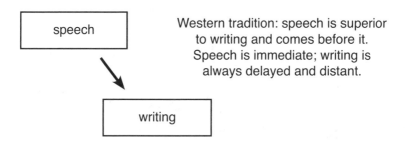

Fig. 1.2. Speech Precedes Writing and Is More Immediate

7. Friedrich Nietzsche, "On Truth and Lies in a Nonmoral Sense," in *Philosophy and Truth: Selections from Nietzsche's Notebooks of the Early 1870s*, trans. and ed. Daniel Breazeale (Atlantic Highlands, NJ: Humanities Press, 1970), 84.

Derrida has sometimes been wrongly understood simply to be reversing the hierarchy between the two terms, putting writing in the place of privilege over speech: "People who are in a bit too much of a hurry have thought that I wasn't interested in the voice, just writing. Obviously, this is not true" (*Poi*, 140). Such a reversal would, to be sure, change the content of the hierarchy, but it would do nothing to challenge or disrupt the hierarchical structure itself. There would still be a privileged and an under-privileged term, which would need deconstructing.

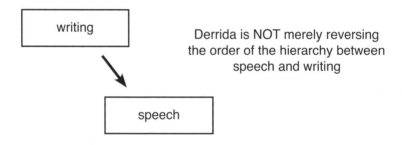

Fig. 1.3. Derrida Is Not Merely Privileging Writing over Speech

Nor does Derrida merely deny any difference whatever between the terms, as if "speech" and "writing" could be used interchangeably:

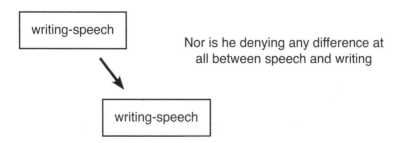

Fig. 1.4. Derrida Is Not Denying Any Difference between Writing and Speech

What Derrida claims instead is that "différance" (spelled "-ance," a term I shall explain presently) is the origin of both speech and writing, but not something outside and separate from them:

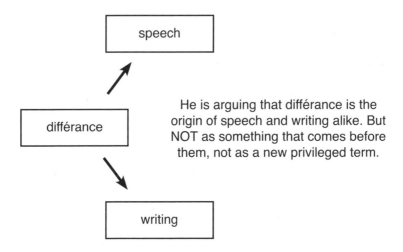

He is arguing that différance is the origin of speech and writing alike. But NOT as something that comes before them, not as a new privileged term.

Fig. 1.5. Différance Does Not Precede Speech and Writing as Their Ground and Origin

Différance does not precede the elements of the opposition it makes possible; it is their mode of existence, just as in traditional Western metaphysics presence itself does not precede that which is present, but rather is the way in which things appear to the godlike consciousness. It is important for us to grasp, therefore, that différance is not a thing in itself, as Derrida stresses:

> What we note as différance will thus be the movement of play that "produces" (and not by something that is simply an activity) these differences, these effects of difference. This does not mean that the différance which produces differences is before them in a simple and in itself unmodified and indifferent present. Différance is the nonfull, nonsimple "origin"; it is the structured and differing origin of differences. (*SP*, 141)

It is also important to grasp that, just as for traditional metaphysics, presence is not just about language, but about the mode of existence of everything that there is (i.e., whatever exists exists in so far as it can be immediately present to my consciousness), so also for Derrida, différance is not just the condition of possibility for language, but for everything one experiences. We could think of presence and différance as the contrast, not between two things, but between two adverbs: according to traditional metaphysics, truth and meaning exist "presently," but according to Derrida, they exist "différantly." Différance is not what there is, but how everything is:

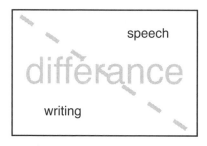

Différance is not a concept that comes before speech and writing in time. It is their condition of possibility, and they exist not so much "within" différance but "as" différance. It is their mode of existence: their existence is one of differing in relation to themselves and to each other.

Fig. 1.6. Différance Is the Mode of Existence of Both Speech and Writing

A further point to make about this final diagram is that we do not first of all experience différance and then fill it with speech and writing—any more than we first experience presence and then fill it with things that are present. The condition of différance is retrojected from our experience of things that exist "différantly."

So then, for Derrida everything that exists exists "différantly," but what is différance? Derrida coined the term différance to indicate that "presence" is always different from itself and deferred with relation to itself. The French verb *différer* can mean both "to differ" and "to defer." Furthermore, by changing the usual spelling of *différence* to *différance*, Derrida introduces a difference that is only discernible in writing, for the two spellings are pronounced identically. This is intended to challenge the idea that meaning is always completely present in speech, but dislocated and distant in writing: in this case the nuance is only discernible in the written form. Elsewhere Derrida calls différance an "arche-writing" (from the Greek *arche*, meaning "beginning" or "origin," French: *archi-écriture*), which is the condition of non-self-presence from which both speech and writing are derived. Arche-writing is not the same as writing-as-opposed-to-speech, and différance is not the same as difference-as-opposed-to-identity; arche-writing is the condition of possibility both of speech and of writing (in other words, it makes them both possible in the first place), and différance is the condition of possibility both of difference and of identity.

Différance, then, is the condition of being according to which "there is no experience of *pure* presence, but only chains of differential marks" (*LI*, 10). In asserting that meaning is a function of difference rather than presence, Derrida is leaning once more on the insights of Saussure. For Saussure, a signifier signifies only because it is different and therefore distinct from other signifiers. We can identify the signifier "cat" within the system of language because it is different from "cot," "bat," "car" and so forth, and indeed because it is different from every other signifier in the language. Identity is derived from difference, rather than difference from identity (remember the binary opposites discussed above, one element of which cannot exist without the other). Similarly, the meaning of signifieds (concepts) is also a function of their place in the whole system of language and their differences from other signifieds. A quick example will help us see how this works. Imagine an Englishwoman and Frenchwoman out for a stroll in the countryside one day. "Just look at that beautiful winding river" exclaims the former excitedly; "Oui, c'est un très beau fleuve," responds the latter. In deciding to use the English word "river," the first speaker had to make a decision about size. The English language differentiates bodies of flowing water in terms of their volume: a river is bigger than a stream, and a stream is bigger than a brook. But the second speaker had a different choice to make: the French language differentiates between water that flows directly into the sea ("un fleuve") or not ("une rivière"). In this example, English and French use different ways of dividing the raw material of reality into concepts, and in both languages the concepts are defined in terms of their differences from other neighboring concepts. No concept is an island entire unto itself, and in order to know its meaning one must know something of the system of which it is an element. In other words, its meaning is not fully present to it, for "no element can function as a sign without referring to another element which itself is not simply present" (*Pos*, 26).

Before we leave this example of rivers and streams, we can note that it also makes Nietzsche's point quite well. Which distinction gives us "the essence of the thing" or the ultimate truth of reality? Rivers/streams, or fleuves/rivières? According to which set of differences does language immediately and exhaustively give us the truth of the world? Are there really rivers and streams, but the benighted French are deluded into using the mistaken distinction of fleuve/rivière, or are our Gallic friends closer to the truth of things with their distinction? The answer, of course, is that neither set of differences gives us the necessary truth of things as they really are, such that we could say all other systems of differences are just wrong. The English language creates the concepts of "rivers" and "streams"; it does not find them out there in the world and then decide to use them, and the same goes for the French "fleuves" and "rivières." Indeed, any number of other systems of differences could be used to create a set of concepts that would be just as adequate for getting on with everyday life.

What does all this mean for Derrida's deconstruction of metaphysics? Expressed starkly, it means: "There is no atom" (*Poi*, 137). That is, meaning and truth are never self-contained, but always rely on their difference from what they are not in order to be what they are. Nothing is ever fully present, because the idea of presence itself is an artificial construct derived from a more originary condition of différance: "Immediacy is derived," and we must speak of "the mirage of the thing itself, of immediate presence, of originary perception" (*OG*, 157). Metaphysics is deconstructed when it is shown that its cherished concepts—presence, immediacy, speech—are not, after all, originary and cannot be defined or understood without that which they seek to brush under the carpet: absence, mediation, writing.

Before we leave this discussion of différance, it is important to make one final observation that will become crucial in the section on ethics. It is that, while Derrida sees the traditional language and concepts of Western metaphysics as an illusion, it is impossible to do away with them completely if we want to say anything intelligible at all. There is no alternative language ready and waiting to be dusted off and employed in the place of metaphysics, and so Derrida must perform the delicate task of deconstructing Western metaphysics from within Western metaphysics, not from some place outside of it (which would be a very metaphysical notion itself, something like Plato's "divine realm" of the Forms [Greek: *topos ouranios*]). Derrida insists that "there is no sense in doing without the concepts of metaphysics in order to shake metaphysics. We have no language—no syntax and no lexicon—which is foreign to this history" (*WD*, 354). So deconstruction always pulls at metaphysics with one foot inside it, rather than critiquing it from the outside.

Deconstruction Is Not Just Another Way of Reading

There is one further misunderstanding of Derrida's work that needs to be corrected before we can move on from this brief survey of his deconstruction of metaphysics. Deconstruction has not infrequently been understood as a method or a way of reading. This is not helped by the way it is often taught in seminars on literary theory: there are Marxist readings of texts, Freudian readings, feminist readings, queer readings, and deconstructive readings. But in the same way that Derrida is careful to say that différance is not some original concept or reality that precedes everything else, he also repeatedly insists that deconstruction is not a method or set of procedures that one can pull off the shelf and set to work on any old unsuspecting text:

> I am wary of the idea of methods of reading. The laws of reading are determined by that particular text that is being read. This does not mean that we should simply abandon ourselves to the text, or represent and repeat it in a purely passive manner. It means that we must remain faithful, even if it implies a certain violence, to the injunctions of the text. These injunctions will differ from one text to the next so that one cannot prescribe one general method of reading. In this sense deconstruction is not a method. (*DCP*, 155)

Why is Derrida so resistant to deconstruction being understood as a method? Because a method brings the same set of tools to everything it encounters: it is a cookie-cutter approach to reading, a one-trick pony that is completely insensitive to the particular text it is reading and just filters the text to find whatever it knew it was looking for before it started reading. With a method, you know what you're going to get. It exploits the text for its own purposes, rather than trying to understand the text in its own terms. This is what Derrida wants to avoid, and it is why he insists that "all sentences of the type 'decon-struction is X' or 'deconstruction is not X' *a priori* miss the point" (LJF, 275). This is also why Derrida keeps changing the terms in which he describes what he is doing: from "deconstruc-tion" and "différance" to "supplementarity," "dissemination," "trace," "pharmakon," "hymen," and "iterability." Each of these terms, though it describes not unrelated moves, comes out of a particular context, out of a particular encounter with a specific text or author, and each term brings different connotations and inflections to Derrida's readings, connotations and inflections that are germane to the particular reading encounters in which they arise.

The changing vocabulary emphasizes that his aim is not to produce a "philosophy of X," (such as a philosophy of literature or a philosophy of science), bringing a preestablished set of static philosophical concepts to whatever he is reading and making every text that he meets fit that same Procrustean bed in a way that keeps his conceptual scheme unscathed and intact through all its encounters. This does not mean there are no tendencies at all in his work, as he points out in an interview:

> I think there are some general rules, some procedures that can be transposed by analogy . . . but these rules are taken up in a text which is each time a unique element and which does not let itself be turned totally into a method. (*Poi*, 200)

Some critics have seen this terminological proliferation as an annoyance, as a lack of clarity or even as pretentious, but for

Derrida it is necessary in order to avoid slipping into methodological predictability. It is for this reason that he is uncomfortable with the term "deconstruction" being used as a general description of his thought (TTP, 44), and it is for this reason that the word "deconstructionism" is never used by Derrida himself. To reduce deconstruction to an ism alongside other isms is to set oneself against everything that Derrida claims about deconstruction.

When Derrida is pressed to define deconstruction—and he does so only with the greatest reluctance—he does so in a way that recalls the framing of différance as an adverb in the discussion above:

> I have often had occasion to define deconstruction as that which is—far from a theory, a school, a method, even a discourse, still less a technique that can be appropriated— at bottom what happens or comes to pass. (TOJ, 17)

Deconstruction, then, is what happens: things deconstruct or, better, things exist deconstructively. As James K. A. Smith elegantly puts it, deconstruction "happens in the middle voice, as it were: ça se déconstruit; it deconstructs itself."[8] So a deconstructive reading of a text, understood in its own terms, is doing nothing more than pointing out the deconstruction that the text was quite happily performing on itself before the reading came along, but that no one had noticed yet. Deconstruction brings nothing to the text apart from a careful, close reading— an analysis that, when it reads thinkers like Plato or Aristotle, "tries to find out how their thinking works or does not work" in order to "find the tensions, the contradictions, the heterogeneity within their own corpus" (*DN*, 9–10). This means that:

8. Smith, *Jacques Derrida*, 9.

> Deconstruction is not an operation that supervenes after-
> wards, from the outside, one fine day. It is always already at
> work in the work. Since the destructive force of deconstruc-
> tion is always already contained within the very architecture
> of the work, all one would finally have to do to be able to
> deconstruct, given this always already, is to do memory work.
> (*MPdM*, 73)

Furthermore, given that deconstruction points something out
that was not previously noticed about how a given text trips over
its own laces, it is not a dry and objective description of how
things exist that leaves those same things just as it found them.
"Deconstruction, I have insisted, is not neutral. It intervenes,"
Derrida asserts (*Pos*, 93). Far from being a detached exercise in
reading, it is "a way of taking a position, in its work of analysis,
concerning the political and institutional structures that make
possible and govern our practices, our competencies, our performances."[9] So we find, as we turn now to consider the ethical
and political import of deconstruction, that we have already been
talking about ethics and politics all along. From the beginning,
Derrida affirms, deconstruction "has done nothing but address"
the problem of justice (FL, 935). In the next section, I will tease
out this interventionist, position-taking dynamic of deconstruction and the ethics and politics to which it gives rise.

9. Jacques Derrida, "The Conflict of Faculties," in *Languages of Knowledge and of Inquiry*, ed. Michael Riffaterre (New York: Columbia University Press, 1982), quoted in Jonathan Culler, *On Deconstruction: Theory and Criticism after Structuralism* (Ithaca, NY: Cornell University Press, 2007), 156.

2

ETHICS AND POLITICS

There was a time when deconstruction was considered to be ethically and politically uncommitted, always deconstructing and hedging around any determinate ethical or political position in a way that leads to paralysis and never allows us to get anything done. This misunderstanding was put to bed in the 1990s by a series of books, prominent among them Simon Critchley's excellent *The Ethics of Deconstruction* (first published 1992),[1] and by a greater willingness on Derrida's part to make the ethical and political dimension of deconstruction more explicit.

The "Mystical Foundation of Authority"

It is not hard to see how the ideas discussed in the previous section are already loaded with ethical and political weight, and much of the Derridean lexicon that we have been exploring in relation to his metaphysics (e.g., identity, purity, difference)

---

1. Simon Critchley, *The Ethics of Deconstruction: Derrida and Levinas*, 3rd ed. (Edinburgh: Edinburgh University Press, 2014).

can be carried directly over into ethical and political registers. In the section on metaphysics, I discussed how binaries like speech and writing do not begin with a stable and unitary origin (immediate and self-present speech), but in a condition that Derrida calls différance or arche-writing, a condition of existence as always different from, and deferred with respect to, itself. This deconstruction of the myth of a pure origin and pure self-presence pertains not only to concepts such as speech and writing, however, but also to more overtly ethical and political binaries.

Consider the origin of political legitimacy and authority, which, in an American context, is traced back to the Constitution and the signing of the Declaration of Independence. Derrida notes that the Declaration of Independence begins with the words "We, the people," yet the people who are said to authorize the declaration are in fact the very group of people that the declaration brings into being. Derrida explains:

> The "we" of the declaration speaks "in the name of the people." But this people does not exist. They do not exist as an entity, it does not exist, before this declaration, not as such. If it gives birth to itself, as free and independent subject, as possible signer, this can hold only in the act of the signature. The signature invents the signer. (DI, 10)

So does the Declaration come first and authorize the creation of "the people," or do the people come first and decide to write the Declaration? Both of these are necessary in order for the declaration to be authoritative, and so we see that its origin is not a unified and triumphant moment, but a temporality split within itself which must, so to speak, go back before its own beginning to authorize itself in what Derrida pithily calls a "mythical retroactivity" ("rétroactivité fabuleuse," DI, 10, translation altered).

Like différance, the moment of the signing of the Declaration is not fully present to itself.

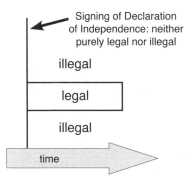

The distinction between "legal" and "illegal" can only come about on the basis of something that is itself neither legal nor illegal, for example the signing of the Declaration of Independence that authorises the creation of a particular legal jurisdiction and justifies itself retroactively.

Fig. 2.1. The Origin of the Distinction between the Legal and the Illegal

So the legality of the law rests on a moment that is itself properly neither legal nor illegal, a moment that needs to be outside the law insofar as it grounds the legitimacy of the law, but which needs to be under the law, lest it itself be illegal. The Declaration of Independence, insofar as it founds the new legal entity of the United States of America, is therefore caught in an "undecidability between . . . a performative structure and a constative structure" (DI, 9). It brings about a new regime of legality (performative), and also vouches for its legitimacy (constative). Everything can be legal or illegal, apart from the law itself (where law is understood not as an isolated statute, but as a constitutional regime of legality), and the law itself can be neither legal nor illegal because it defines what is to be counted as legal and illegal. This is what Derrida, quoting Pascal in "Force of Law," calls the "mystical foundation of authority" (FL, 238–40).

Not Relativism but Incommensurability

As we press further into Derrida's ethical and political thought, we need to deal with an accusation that has often been made against him: that of relativism. In fact, we shall see that dealing with this objection is a good way of getting to the heart of what Derrida says about ethics and politics. Imagine you are playing a game with a young girl. You take turns choosing two objects at random, and the other player has to make a comparison between them, either silly or serious. You start by giving the child an easy example: "I choose the number two and the number three." Pleased as punch, she immediately comes up with a relative comparison: "That's easy: two is smaller than three." As the game continues, she tries to get more adventurous: "I choose . . . a chair and an elephant." "Let's say," you reply, "that a chair and an elephant both have four legs," hoping that she doesn't remember the swivel chair she saw in your office the other day. After a few more predictable rounds, she comes up with a comparison that really stumps you. "Okay, I give you the number two and this table," she says, thumping the table with her little hand. As you try to think of something that an abstract number has in common with this concrete particular, you try to exude an air of calm. But your mind races: it won't do to say that there is only one table, because that will be a comparison between the table and there being one or two of something, rather than with the number two itself. You can't say that the number two is greater than the table, nor can you say it is fewer than the table. You can't say that the table is heavier than the number two, bigger than the number two, or newer than the number two. In fact, you eventually have to concede that there is no common measure that can do justice both to the table and to the number two in their own terms. However, being a proud adult, you decide, rather than admitting defeat, to change the subject and put on the child's favorite DVD, hoping that her victory will soon be forgotten.

This imaginary game helps us to understand what Derrida means when he insists that "I am no relativist," because the term describes a "way of referring to the absolute and denying it" (HJR, 78). In order to hold that two things are relative, we need to have a common measure that can do justice to them both. In other words, it needs to make sense to speak of the two things as having something in common. For example, the numbers two and three are relative to each other because, both being numbers, they can be measured against each other. A chair and a table share common elements of structure, volume, craftsmanship, and color. If Derrida were saying that all judgments are judgments of this sort, then deconstruction would indeed be a sort of relativism. But this is not what Derrida is saying. In fact, it is diametrically opposed to what he is saying. He does not claim that everything is relative, and therefore that the comparisons we make between them are relative judgments. He claims that things are incommensurable, and that it is impossible to make comparisons between them that do proper justice to them. Making ethical judgments for Derrida is like trying to compare the number two with a table in a way that does justice to both elements of the comparison. If the two things were relative, then there would be no problem; the difficulty for Derrida's ethics is precisely that there can be no relativism.

"Every Other Is Wholly Other"

Derrida's own way of putting this incommensurability of one thing to another is that "every other is wholly other," or, slightly clumsier, that "every other (one) is every (bit) other," which both translate the French "tout autre est tout autre" (see, for example, *GD*, 77). He first uses the phrase in his discussion of Kierkegaard in *The Gift of Death* (first published in French in 1992). The gift in question is Abraham's near-sacrifice of his son Isaac on Mount Moriah in Genesis 22. If Abraham had merely followed the rules of conventional morality, Kierkegaard argues, then he would never have been ready to go through with sacrificing his son. (Whether or not this is a correct understanding of the ethics of Abraham's time is not our concern here; I happen to think it would have been quite in line with what the neighbors were doing). When Abraham hears God's voice commanding him to sacrifice Isaac, he must set aside all his rational qualms and questions (how can God's promise be fulfilled if Isaac, the son of the promise, is dead?) in order to obey the absolute injunction that exceeds his ability to assimilate it to conventional codes of ethics.

While Derrida takes care to stress that we are not all like Abraham, in the sense that we are to go and sacrifice our children if someone tells us to do so, he does nevertheless discern in Abraham's experience something that is common to all decisions. When Abraham "accepts his responsibility by heading off towards the absolute request of the other, beyond knowledge," his action highlights "the paradoxical condition of every decision: it cannot be deduced from a form of knowledge of which it would simply be the effect, conclusion or explication" (*GD*, 77). Why not? Because such a "decision" would be merely an automated exercise in following rules, for which no real thinking is required, and not a real decision at all. It is in this sense that Derrida affirms:

> What can be said about Abraham's relation to God can be said about my relation without relation to every other (one) as every (bit) other [*tout autre comme tout autre*],

in particular my relation to my neighbor or my loved ones who are as inaccessible to me, as secret and transcendent as Jahweh. (*GD*, 78)

Every other is just as singular, just as unique, as God, and their words deserve just as much careful weighing. In order to understand the ethical weight of "every other is wholly other," consider the following scenario. Think of the person who means the most to you in the world. It might be a parent, a child, or a cherished friend. Now ask yourself: how much money is that person's life worth? Would you put the value at around a million dollars, or perhaps ten million? More? Perhaps they would be worth more because they are young, or worth less because they have a terminal illness. How much money would it take for you to be willing to part with them?

What quickly becomes clear in any such line of questioning (I hope!) is that there is no answer to the question in the terms in which it is posed. It is not about the numerical value, for attaching any monetary sum to human life has something repulsive and uncomfortable about it. My grandmother is not worth *n* million dollars to me, even if the value in question is all the money in the world. People are singular, irreplaceable, and their existence is outside the bartering and haggling of the market. In the same way, deconstruction seeks to respect singularity, not only in human beings, but also in judgments and comparisons in general. Things cannot blithely be reduced to a measure of general equivalence, because that would rob them of their singularity, their uniqueness.

Language and Violence

Let us now move on and think not in terms of dollars, but in terms of language. Just like the monetary economy, language is a system of equivalence. A given word can refer to lots of different things in the world. The word *dog*, for example, has not been specifically crafted for one unique canine in the history of the world, but applies to a whole class of animals. The word is reusable, or what Derrida calls "iterable," from the Latin *iter*, meaning "again," and the Sanskrit *itara*, meaning "other": it is endlessly repeatable, but each repetition is in a new context and therefore not absolutely identical with any previous iteration—hence "other." It is this otherness in iterability that distinguishes it from a classically philosophical "universal." A given dog, however—say Tammy, my wife's childhood Labrador—is not a universal, but a particular. There was and will ever be only one Tammy (even though there have no doubt been many dogs called "Tammy" over the course of history). Now, when I describe a singular thing (Tammy) in terms of an iterable or universal term ("dog") in such a way that I give the impression that I have said all that there is to say about her, Derrida condemns my language as part of "the violence of difference, of classification, and of the system of appellations" (*OG*, 110). It is violent because I have betrayed the uniqueness of the singular thing in reducing it to an iterable signifier. I have dared "to think the unique within the system, to inscribe it there," which for Derrida is "the gesture of arche-writing: arche-violence, loss of the proper, of absolute proximity, of self-presence" (*OG*, 112). I have presumed to speak on its behalf before all the data is in, without having the exhaustive knowledge of all relevant contexts that would ensure that I could say "this declaration is correct" or "this judgment is just." It is as if I am saying that one dog is just as good as any other because the word "dog" will do just fine for all of them. This might not seem such a terrible crime, but let's raise the stakes a little. Rather than having "dog" as our iterable concept, how about "Jew" in 1930s Germany or "Negro" in the early twentieth-century Deep South. It is not hard to see how such iterable concepts can very quickly cover over shades of difference and complexity and lead to mistreatment and abuse.

It is worth pointing out that this sensitivity to singularity shines forth, not only in Derrida's writing on ethical themes, but also in his own reading encounters:

> I almost never wrote on this or that author *in general*, nor did I treat the totality of a corpus as if it were homogeneous. What is important to me is rather the distribution of forces and motifs in a given work, and to recognize what is hegemonic in it or what is given secondary importance or is even denied. There, too, I tried—and I strive to do this in every case—to respect the idiom or the singularity of the signature. (*FWT*, 7)

If we are to understand why Derrida writes about ethics and politics in the way he does, it is important that we feel the weight of the ethical obligation to which his thought is seeking to respond. Consider for a moment Western twentieth-century history, the context in which Derrida is writing. Consider the nationalism that led to the First World War, the ideologies of racial purity and sexual degeneracy that haunted the death camps of the Second, or the ethnic cleansing that continued to rumble on as the century drew to a close. Consider the painfully unravelling and never fully unraveled legacy of Western colonialism and the excruciatingly slow enfranchisement of adult women, granted in France only in 1944. The twentieth century is a catalogue of ways in which categories of inclusion and exclusion, of "us" and "them," sent the West stumbling from one catastrophe or disgrace to another. It is not unreasonable, given such a litany, that tribalism, fixed identities, and the uncompromising policing of the border between the "inside" and the "outside" are understood as the most damaging and destructive

ethical and political dangers, and therefore why disrupting such
boundaries is a profoundly politically committed thing to do.
On a smaller scale, no doubt we have all, at one time or another,
been annoyed at being "pigeonholed" by someone who assumes
that we must necessarily think or act in a particular way because
of our gender, our family background, our religion, or some
other feature. Language, for Derrida, can be understood as a
generalized pigeonholing. In fact, the example of "dog" might
not be too far from this violence after all, for today many people (including Derrida in his later writing) see the distinction
between human and animal as providing the same sort of excuse
for exploitation as the binary of black and white or male and
female did in past generations: animals are not humans, so it is
okay to kill and eat them.

So far I have sketched one half of Derrida's ethics: iterable
language is violent when it seeks to speak about singular or
unique things. The second half, which the reader may well have
thought of already as an objection to what I have said so far, is
that it is no solution simply to stop using language at all for fear
of doing violence. Let us return for a moment to our example of
the monetary value of a human life. Even if we are agreed that
there is something uncomfortable about putting a finite dollar
value on a singular human existence, we cannot avoid making
that sort of decision as a society when we distribute funds for
the provision of healthcare. Will we allocate our finite pot of
money to curing this disease or to caring for that group of people? Should we put just as much money into saving the life of a
hundred-year-old whose prognosis is to die within the year no
matter what we do, as we would to save the life of a baby who
may have one hundred years to live? We may not like having to
make that sort of decision, but a refusal to allocate the money
would mean that they will both die. The ethical injunction to
do something with the money is absolute and immediate, but we

can never be completely at ease and blasé about any particular way we choose to allocate the funds. There is a certain violence inherent in a particular allocation of funds—the violence of letting some die, while others live—but there is a greater violence in refusing to help anyone, just because there is no perfect way to care for everyone.

Derrida calls this inability to avoid violence a "double bind": I must make a decision, but any decision I make will leave me culpable and, so to speak, with blood on my hands. The decision is "undecidable," which means that there is no fail-safe way to punch some numbers into a calculator to determine the best decision to make in a way that no one could ever criticize or question. I cannot calculate the value of lives against each other, but I must. This is the point that Derrida made in a paper on justice delivered at the Cardozo Law School in 1989 and later printed under the title "Force of Law":

> The undecidable is not merely the oscillation or the tension between two decisions; it is the experience of that which, though heterogeneous, foreign to the order of the calculable and the rule, is still obliged—it is of obligation that we must speak—to give itself up to the impossible decision, while taking account of laws and rules. A decision that did not go through the ordeal of the undecidable would not be a free decision, it would only be the programmable application or unfolding of a calculable process. It might be legal; it would not be just. (FL, 252)

Notice in this passage that to say that a decision is "undecidable" does not mean that it does not matter, or that it could equally go either way without making much difference. It is precisely because the decision does matter that it is undecidable. A judgment is undecidable when I can never be in possession of all the relevant facts that I would need to make it, so that I can be completely confident and satisfied that I have, beyond all possibility of doubt, made a just judgment. Rather than simply posing a problem for Derrida's ethics, such undecidability (or what, elsewhere, he calls the aporia of the decision, from the Greek *a-poros*, that which one cannot pass through) makes ethics into something more than the blind and unthinking following of rules:

> If I know what to do, well, I would apply the rule, and teach my students to apply the rule. But would that be ethical? I'm not sure. I would consider this unethical. Ethics start when you don't know what to do, when there is this gap between knowledge and action, and you have to take responsibility for inventing the new rule which doesn't yet exist. (FT, 152, translation altered)

In order to understand how the undecidable works for Derrida, we need to note his distinction in this passage between law (*droit* in French) and justice (*justice* in French). The law is that which is codified, categorized, and calculated: a system of rules that can be laid down in black and white. But merely adhering to the letter of the law, as we know from the excuse of the war criminal that "I was just following orders," is in itself not enough, and often is not just. If decisions are always simply calculated, then there is never any hope of changing anything, never any hope of uncovering injustice. Each case is treated as though it were just the same as all the rest, and judgments are pumped out like sausages from a sausage factory. In one final analogy, sticking with calculation is like dressing runway models in off-the-rack clothes: nothing fits properly, and the trained eye can see that care has not been taken.

So with law there is just robotic obedience. A judgment

that simply measures a case against the codified law will never be a just judgment, taking into account the singularity of the case. Justice, on the other hand, is singular, and for that reason it cannot be codified. It is, in Derrida's words, "foreign to the order of the calculable and the rule." It takes into account all the complexities and all the context of the singular case. One might legitimately say, "I am lawful" when following a particular rule, but one can never claim with absolute confidence that "I am just." "One cannot speak directly about justice, thematize or objectivize justice, say 'this is just,' and even less 'I am just,' without immediately betraying justice" (FL, 237). Justice goes beyond calculable law, but it is not completely unrelated to it. The relation between law and justice is not a zero-sum game. Calculation is certainly not sufficient to arrive at justice, but it is necessary, and Derrida is by no means advocating that we stop thinking carefully and simply flip a coin or decide on gut instinct.

The structure sketched here in relation to (calculable) law and (absolute) justice is repeated by Derrida in a number of different ways elsewhere in his work. He writes, for instance, about a calculating, parsimonious hospitality that is always asking what is the least it can get away with to keep up appearances, and an "absolute" or "unconditional hospitality," which welcomes all strangers and asks no questions. He writes about reciprocal gift-giving, in which I carefully calculate the expense of the gift I need to give, in return for the one I have received, in order to keep up appearances. He then contrasts this to the true gift, which is given without the expectation of receiving anything in return, and which, at its purest, is not even acknowledged as a gift by the giver or the receiver. If it were so acknowledged, then the giver would begin "to pay himself with a symbolic recognition, to praise himself, to approve of himself, to gratify himself, to congratulate himself, to give back to himself symbolically the value of what he thinks he has given or what he is preparing to give" (*GT*, 14). If we give out of duty or because we think it is expected, because it is due, then we are not really giving a gift. Most of us, no doubt, can remember how it felt to give or receive a token "gift" that was offered just for the sake of having something to give. In the table below, I list some more examples of similar contrasts in Derrida's work between the absolute and the calculating or conditional:

THEME	ABSOLUTE	CONDITIONAL	DERRIDA'S TEXT
Hospitality	Unconditional, absolute hospitality; absolute surprise	Conditional, predicted, and calculated hospitality	*Of Hospitality*
The gift	The absolute, unrecognized, and unreciprocated gift	Gift as part of a calculated economy of reciprocation	*Given Time; The Gift of Death*
Forgiveness	Forgiving the unforgivable	Forgiving the forgivable	*On Cosmopolitanism and Forgiveness*
Mourning	Unconditional mourning	Conditional mourning	*The Work of Mourning*
Responsibility	Hyperbolic, excessive responsibility; absolute responsibility to the singular demand of the other	Limited, circumscribed responsibility; behavior according to a general rule	*The Gift of Death*
Justice	The singularity of the case	The general categories of the law	"Force of Law"

Time	Time out of joint; radically open to the coming of the other; messianic	Time as an extrapolation and outworking of those factors present from the beginning; more of the same	*Specters of Marx*
Paying respect	Adding to, critiquing, or dislocating the ideas of the one to whom one pays respect, making them in some way other to themselves	Simply repeating the ideas or words of the one to whom one is paying respect, without changing anything	*Adieu to Emmanuel Levinas*
Decision	An "impossible" decision, incalculable and unmasterable	The calculating, predictable decision that could not have been otherwise: not a real decision	"Force of Law"
Invention	The uninventible	The inventible	"Psyche: Invention of the Other" in *Psyche: Inventions of the Other*
Democracy	Monstrous democra-cy-to-come	Existing democ-racies or future democracies in linear continuity with the present (predictable)	*Rogues: Two Essays on Reason*

In each of these cases, the absolute, pure, or unconditional version of the motif in question is unattainable. I can never give the pure gift, make the absolutely just decision, or exhaust my hyperbolic responsibility to the other. These are unconditional and inaccessible, and they cannot be brought within the circulation of meanings in language and are therefore not amenable to deconstruction. So Derrida can write in "Force of Law," for example, that "justice in itself, if there is such a thing, outside or beyond law, is not deconstructible" (FL, 243, translation altered). He has to add "if there is such a thing" (French "s'il y en a") because justice cannot be designated as a concept or a signified, the meaning of which can be presented to consciousness as a "there is"/"il y a," evoking again the Heideggerian "there is" that we discussed in relation to "there is nothing outside the text" above.

Derrida of course is not suggesting that, for example, all our gift-giving should be of the pure and absolute kind; indeed, he is arguing that this would be impossible. But neither is he saying that, because it is impossible, we should not even attempt to give in a way that is more than a proxy for self-gratification. We should not stop giving gifts because no gift is pure, in the same way that we should not remain in complete silence because all language is violent. The absolute or the impossible gift haunts all gift-giving, the impossible decision haunts all calculative judgments, absolute hospitality haunts all conditional acts of hospitality, and so forth. These impossible notions remain before us as reminders that even our best gift-giving is never free from a self-serving desire for recognition, that our best attempts at justice are fallible approximations, or that, in Isaiah's terms, "all our righteous deeds are like a polluted garment" (Isa. 64:6).

How might we sum up the tenor or thrust of Derrida's intervention here, in order to try to characterize his ethics and politics in general (though he would no doubt be annoyed with us doing so)? We could say this: Derrida is always against resting on our ethical or political laurels, thinking that we have all the knotty problems solved and all the loose ends tied up and that there is no more hard thinking to do. He is against following established rules and conventions without considering on each occasion whether those rules or conventions are themselves just. He is always against authority setting itself up as unimpeachable or natural, and he incessantly exposes its contingent or artificial origins.

3

THEOLOGY

We already have almost all the ideas and concepts in place to understand Derrida's relation to theology. We have seen that he rejects the sufficiency of the merely determinate and calculable, and that he insists upon the necessity (but also the impossibility) of the absolute, unconditional, or incalculable. We have seen that he seeks to disrupt self-identical origins, especially when they act as the foundation for claims to authority. We have seen how he considers language incapable of capturing the uniqueness of singular beings. These themes are developed further as we now explore some of the most important aspects of Derrida's ideas about theology.

In his writings of the late 1960s onward, Derrida consistently engaged with themes from the Western theological tradition. We noted above how, in *Of Grammatology*, he considers the Western understanding of signification to be irreducibly theological in that it relies on a transcendental signified. In addition to his treatment of Kierkegaard in *The Gift of Death*, Derrida tackles the notion of faith (in relation to Kant) in "Faith and Knowledge," and his "Circumfession" is a personal and intimate reflection on, and reflection of, Augustine's *Confessions*. We can find a way into the different themes raised in these texts by beginning with a consideration of what Derrida says about himself in relation to God.

"I Rightly Pass for an Atheist"

Perhaps his most famous pronouncement on the subject of theology is his affirmation in "Circumfession" that "the constancy of God in my life is called by other names, so that I quite rightly pass for an atheist" (C, 155). Why this form of words? Why not simply say, "I am an atheist," and be done with it? For the very good reason that theism/atheism is just the sort of binary opposition that Derrida persistently deconstructs. To claim that "I am an atheist" is just as totalizing, just as much of a hubristic claim to be in possession of all the relevant cosmic facts, as a dogmatic claim to theism. To affirm that one is an atheist in this sense (in the sense that it claims to know the ultimate truth about the universe with certainty) is a very religious claim to make. Theism is obsessed with presence and the origin, and atheism is just as obsessed with there being no presence or origin; dogmatic atheism is just as dogmatic as dogmatic theism. In the same way that Derrida is not content simply to invert the hierarchy of speech and writing, he is not content to opt straightforwardly for atheism over theism. Simply to reject the theism/atheism binary out of hand, however, would be an attempt to leave metaphysics in one decisive leap, which would itself be a metaphysical move (because metaphysics is the logic of absolute breaks and ruptures). Here, as elsewhere, Derrida does not claim to be able to move beyond problematic binaries altogether, but he destabilizes (or deconstructs) their emphatic dichotomy. This does not mean that Derrida is an agnostic, equally open to the possibility of the existence or nonexistence of the God of the Bible. Such a claim to agnosticism is too weak for Derrida because, as he insists in *Positions*, différance "blocks every relationship to theology" (*Pos*, 40). In other words, there cannot be both an irreconcilable differing and deferring at the origin of all identity and the God of traditional Christian theology.

This structural incompatibility of the biblical God and différance shows why we must be careful not to isolate Derridean ideas and graft them into a Christian register, for in so doing we do an injustice both to the Bible and to Derrida. For instance, when James K. A. Smith argues that Derrida's *il n'y a pas de hors-texte* "can be considered a radical translation of the Reformation principle *sola scriptura*,"[1] his argument needs to bracket or elide the difference between the Creator-creature distinction and the différance that "blocks every relation to theology" and to smooth over the difference between a means of revelation of the absolute, personal God and the condition of all being in a universe explicitly without any transcendent God. *Sola scriptura* does not imply or require that the condition of all meaning is textual, and Derrida's insight does not "push us to recover . . . the centrality of scripture for mediating our understanding of the world as a whole,"[2] unless "scripture" means all textuality irrespective of traditional canon, which it does not. Christians do not need Derrida to remind them of *sola scriptura*, not least because *sola scriptura* is not what he reminds them of. In his brief comparison of *il n'y a pas de hors texte* and *sola scriptura*, Smith makes a number of elisions, concatenations, and jumps that are indicative of a wider trend in some Christian scholarship of seeking too eagerly to appropriate the "Egyptian loot" of postmodern thought for Christian purposes.[3] Such approaches

---

1. James K. A. Smith, *Who's Afraid of Postmodernism?: Taking Derrida, Lyotard, and Foucault to Church* (Grand Rapids: Baker Academic, 2006), 23.
2. Ibid., 23.
3. Ibid., 22.

locate superficial or rhetorical similarities between postmodern thinkers and the Bible, but these similarities crumble when they are considered in the context of the deeper differences between the two positions.

It has been suggested by some, furthermore, that Derrida's thought functions something like a negative theology, incessantly speaking around the divine and saying what God is not, as a roundabout way of talking about God without saying anything definite about him. But negative theology, Derrida argues in "Différance," maintains an idea of God as a pure presence that can be experienced in mystical union beyond language, whereas Derrida holds to no such mystical possibility. It has even been suggested that différance itself functions as a deity for Derrida, but he is quite emphatic in stating that it "is not an ineffable Being which no name could approach: God, for example" (*MP*, 26). As we saw in the section on metaphysics above, différance is not anything in itself, but the way in which everything exists. I cannot see how this could be construed as a deity.

The God of Ontotheology

To deconstruct the metaphysics of presence is to deconstruct God, or more specifically what Derrida, following Heidegger, calls the God of ontotheology. It is to the exploration of ontotheology that we now turn, as we ask, "In which God does Derrida not believe?" Heidegger coined the term ontotheology (from the Greek *ontos*, meaning "being"; *theos*, meaning "God"; and *logos*, here meaning "study") to designate the study of god as the highest being. He uses the term primarily in relation to Aristotle's divine Unmoved Mover, the first principle of the Aristotelian universe. In his seminars from 1956–57, published under the title *Identity and Difference*, Heidegger names this supreme Aristotelian being the *causa sui* ("the cause of itself," i.e., the self-sufficient one, uncaused by anything outside itself): "This is the appropriate name for the god of philosophy. Man cannot pray to this god, nor offer sacrifices to him. Man cannot fall to his knees in awe before the *causa sui*, nor dance and play music before this god."[4] So the god of ontotheology is a concept-god, an impersonal principle necessary to facilitate a particular understanding of being, according to which everything has a cause and all causes can be traced back to god, the uncaused cause. It is the god ridiculed by Blaise Pascal as "the god of the philosophers" in his *Mémorial*, a text found stitched into the lining of his clothing at his death: "GOD of Abraham, GOD of Isaac, GOD of Jacob, not of the philosophers and of the learned." For our purposes, it is important to note that the god of ontotheology makes reality coherent (for everything has a cause), unified (for all causes can be traced back to the *causa sui*, the Unmoved Mover, and this god is itself unitary and undivided), and well-founded (for the *causa sui* is the metaphysical ground or foundation of all beings).

Ontotheology brings Aristotle's Prime Mover into the Christian tradition, "baptizing" Aristotle and, in so doing, pressing Christian doctrine into an unbiblical, Aristotelian mold. In an illuminating fragment from "Structure, Sign, and Play in the Discourse of the Human Sciences," we can clearly see that, for Derrida, "God" is one way among many of expressing the idea of presence and unity, a presence that may be called "essence, existence, substance, subject . . . transcendentality, consciousness, God, man, and so forth" (*WD*, 353). When Derrida deconstructs self-presence and self-identicality, he is also inevitably deconstructing the Unmoved Mover, the god of ontotheology. In other words, the god of ontotheology is to theology what the metaphysics of presence is to metaphysics: a

---

4. Martin Heidegger, *Identity and Difference*, trans. J. Stambaugh (New York: Harper & Row, 1969), 72.

rationally exhaustible self-presence that guarantees the stability of the system of concepts that it governs.

Where Derrida is distinctive in his account of ontotheology is in his denial that we can ever escape it fully. In a discussion of Heidegger's destruction of metaphysics, Derrida insists on the difficulty of leaving metaphysics behind definitively, in the statement already quoted above: "There is no sense in doing without the concepts of metaphysics in order to shake metaphysics. We have no language—no syntax and no lexicon—which is foreign to this history" (*WD*, 354). He elaborates on this by insisting that attempts to escape ontotheology once and for all are "trapped in a circle" (*WD*, 354). Why? Because ontotheology itself is characterized by its insistence on absolute breaks: God is absolutely transcendent and absolutely self-sufficient and self-contained. To insist on an absolute break with ontotheology, therefore, is to seek to vanquish ontotheology in a very ontotheological way: the loser wins. In Derrida's own words: "We can pronounce not a single destructive proposition which has not already had to slip into the form, the logic, and the implicit postulations of precisely what it seeks to contest" (*WD*, 354). Translated into more biblical language, we might say that the god of ontotheology is an idol of completeness and self-sufficiency, but to assume to vanquish the idol with one clean blow is to see it rise from its ashes in the form of one's own self-sufficient and complete victory.

Messianicity without Messianism

In his thinking, Derrida seeks to retain certain formal, structural features of theology while removing their determinate biblical content. He commonly expresses this with the motif of "x without x," such as "religion without religion," "God without God," or "messianicity without messianism." In this section, I will focus on messianism, but by considering messianicity in

Derrida's thought, the reader will appreciate the privileging of structure over determinate content that runs through each of Derrida's "x without x" motifs.

Messianism, as Derrida understands it, can be either religious or secular. His main religious reference is Jewish messianism, the hope for the future appearing of God's anointed one, who will bring justice and peace on earth and restore the fortunes of God's people. The present is lived in expectation of the future time when messianic prophecy will be fulfilled.

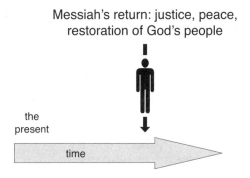

Fig. 3.1. Jewish Messianism

The primary secular messianism, as far as Derrida is concerned, is to be found in Marx's philosophy of history, according to which the inevitable proletarian revolution will bring about, after a period of the dictatorship of the proletariat, a classless society of justice and peace. As in the case of Jewish messianism, the present is lived in confident expectation of the inevitable future overturning of fortunes.

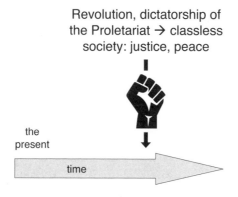

Fig. 3.2. Marxian Messianism

Both of these messianisms have a determinate content: we know what will happen to bring justice and peace (the coming of Yahweh's Messiah or the overthrow of the capitalist system by a proletarian revolution). But in terms of his own thinking, what Derrida offers is not this or that determinate messianism, but what he calls "messianicity without messianism," a "structural messianism," or again a messianism "which I regard as a universal structure of experience, and which cannot be reduced to religious messianism of any stripe" (MS, 248). He seeks to maintain the expectation of a future overturning of the status quo (i.e., "messianicity") without ascribing that change to any determinate agent (i.e., "without messianism"). Derrida retains the structure of the promise of something to come, an "endless promise" (TSI, 38), in that it can never be co-opted or reduced to any particular determinate content. What will come is not any named messiah, but "the most irreducibly heterogeneous otherness" (MS, 249), which means that whatever it is that comes, it will certainly not be what, or who, we are expecting. As for the state that this advent will bring about, Derrida describes it as the "democracy to come," by which he does not mean the linear prolongation into the future of contemporary systems of parliamentary and representative democracy, but a disruptive, nonlinear "event" that is unforeseeable, unexpected, and—like justice in "Force of Law"—impossible:

> The event must also announce itself as im-possible; it must thus announce itself without calling in advance, without fore-warning, announcing itself without announcing itself, with-out any horizon of expectation, any telos, formation, form, or teleological preformation. Whence its always monstrous, unpresentable character, demonstrable as un-monstrable. (R, 144)

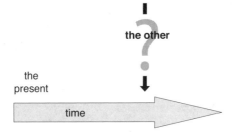

Democracy to come (other, unpredictable, unforeseeable, unexpected): peace, justice

the other

the present

time

Derrida seeks to keep the structure of messianicity in general but to empty it of any particular determinate content. His own "democracy to come" promises perfect freedom and perfect equality, but such a regime is unimaginable. This promise will never become a here-and-now reality.

Fig. 3.3. Messianicity without Messianism

This figure of the monstrous parallels Derrida's insistence on the justice that exceeds all calculable law. If we could predict what is to come, then it would no longer be radically other to what already exists, but an event within the current horizon of expectation, and it is this calculability of the future that Derrida wants to avoid at all costs: "A future that would not be monstrous would not be a future; it would already be a predictable, calculable, and programmable tomorrow" (*Poi*, 387). Derrida does specify that the democracy to come will bring about the impossible concurrent realization of absolute freedom (and singularity) and absolute equality (and equivalence). Freedom and equality are both necessary for democracy, but also contradictory because equality demands that people be thought of as equivalent, and freedom that they be thought of as singular.

The evocation of freedom and equality means that, though the advent of the democracy to come will be monstrous, it is not radically indeterminate. If another Hitler-like figure were to come, for example, with a National Socialist ideology of Aryan supremacy, Derrida would have no hesitation at all in affirming that the figure is not that for which he was waiting. The "to come" will surprise our expectations, but it will not surprise the deconstructive expectation of surprise.

So what, then, are we to make of this absolute freedom and equality? Is this Derrida smuggling some determinacy back into his supposedly indeterminate ethics and politics? Is the universal "democracy to come" in fact a badly disguised reworking of the freedom and equality of French republicanism? Some have certainly thought so, arguing that if the monstrous thing to come is truly other and unpredictable, then it must be possible for it to be evil and despotic just as much as benevolent and benign, and "what I welcome as a vital chance may turn out to be a lethal threat."[5] Derrida does have a response to such criticism, however. Take the example of Hitler again: his ideology introduces a series

---

5. Martin Hägglund, *Radical Atheism: Derrida and the Time of Life* (Stanford: Stanford University Press, 2008), 31.

of determinations, divisions, and categories: Jew and Gentile, Aryan and non-Aryan, and so on, and therefore it sets itself up directly against the indeterminacy that Derrida is seeking to place at the heart of his ethics and politics. The absolute freedom and absolute equality of which Derrida speaks, by contrast, introduce no distinctions between different groups of people (or, as some of his later work explores, no fixed and rigid distinctions between humans and "non-human" animals, either), and so it could be argued that it enacts, on the level of political content, the indeterminacy and openness that Derrida prizes. All are to be equal without distinction; all are to be free without distinction. Of all possible political systems, it could be argued, the democracy to come is the least determinate and prescriptive.

One further feature of the democracy to come which distinguishes it, at least in theory, from both Jewish and Marxist messianisms, is that there is a recognition on Derrida's part that such democracy will never fully come:

> For democracy remains to come; this is its essence insofar as it remains: not only will it remain indefinitely perfectible, hence always insufficient and future, but, belonging to the time of the promise, it will always remain, in each of its future times, to come. (*PF*, 306)

The democracy to come will never be realized perfectly, and it functions (like justice) as a constant, absolute demand to think again about freedom and equality, and to make them dovetail better than they do at present. One way in which Derrida talks of the unbridgeable futurity of the democracy to come is that structural messianicity "overflows" every determinate messianism.

We can discern in this motif of "x without x" another instance of a move with which we are by now familiar. In the same way that différance is the condition of possibility of both speech and writing, here Derrida is searching for something more generic than any determinate religion, which serves as the structural condition of possibility for all determinate religions (though in practical terms his concern is for the Abrahamic religions, and for Judaism and Christianity in particular). His assumption is that particular religions, particular gods, and particular messianisms partake of structures more fundamental than any of their determinate instances, structures from which the determinate content can be removed in order to leave philosophically serviceable patterns of thought.

PART 2

A REFORMED ASSESSMENT OF DERRIDA'S THOUGHT

In addressing these issues, why don't these men deal with Van Til?
It is all there in Van Til. Here is a bumper sticker:
"Van Til, now more than ever!"[1]

Derrida's reception within the broad tradition of Christian thought is as varied as that tradition itself, ranging from, on the one side, the argument that his thinking and the thought of others like him must form the basis of the "next Reformation," without which the church will wither and die,[2] to, on the other side, denunciation of deconstruction as "the critical method which virtually declares that the identity and intentions of the

---

1. Doug Wilson, "Pretending to Leave Modernity Behind," review of *Who's Afraid of Postmodernism?* by James K. A. Smith, available at dougwils.com/books /pretending-to-leave-modernity-behind.html (accessed January 13, 2016).

2. See Carl Raschke, *The Next Reformation: Why Evangelicals Must Embrace Postmodernity* (Grand Rapids: Baker Academic, 2004).

author of a text are irrelevant to the interpretation of the text, prior to insisting that no meaning can be found in it."[3] The first approach comes only to praise Derrida, the second only to bury him, and neither is adequate.

---

3. Alastair E. McGrath, *Christian Theology: An Introduction,* 2nd ed. (Oxford: Basil Blackwell, 1995), 114.

4

DERRIDA AND VAN TIL: A CHAPTER WAITING TO BE WRITTEN

Space does not permit here an encyclopedic survey of the ways in which Derrida's thought has been received across the Christian traditions, and it is not the purpose of this series to provide such overviews. I will address some of Derrida's more important Christian readers in the course of the reflections below and in the bibliography at the end of this book, and I direct the interested reader to chapter 7 of Steven Shakespeare's *Derrida and Theology*.[1] In these pages, I will confine myself to engagement with Derrida's philosophy by Reformed thinkers in what has come to be known as "presuppositionalist" or "Van Tilian" thought, a tradition out of which relatively little engagement with Derrida has come.[2]

1. Steven Shakespeare, "Gift or Poison? Theological Responses to Derrida," in *Derrida and Theology* (London: T & T Clark, 2009), 175–208.
2. Doug Wilson, "Pretending to Leave Modernity Behind," review of *Who's Afraid of Postmodernism?* by James K. A. Smith, available at dougwils.com/books

One notable exception is the article "Derrida, Van Til and the Metaphysics of Postmodernism,"[3] which helpfully maps out of some of the similarities and differences between the two thinkers, particularly in relation to the difference between personal and impersonal principles.

Frame's Reformed Readings
and Misreadings of Derrida

Before I provide, as this series dictates, a "Reformed assessment" of Derrida's thought with a Van Tilian flavor and, above all, a biblical basis, I think it will be helpful to discuss at some length the engagement with Derrida's ideas by one prominent Reformed thinker: John Frame. It is my aim in doing so to help to correct many of the mistakes that Reformed and other readers of Derrida have often made in interpreting him. I am not singling Frame out as a particularly bad reader of Derrida, nor as a bad philosopher. Quite to the contrary, much of what I have to say in the rest of this book is deeply indebted to Frame's thought, and he mentions Derrida only in passing, so it would be unreasonable to treat these occasional mentions with the same rigor as if he had written a book on Derrida. Nevertheless, Frame does express a number of infelicitous interpretations of Derrida that are widespread and which, therefore, it is prudent to highlight and discuss.

Frame most often discusses Derrida together with other late twentieth-century thinkers under the banner of "postmodernism," arguing that "the views of postmodernists like Lyotard and

---

/pretending-to-leave-modernity-behind.html (accessed January 13, 2016).

3. Jacob Gabriel Hale, "Derrida, Van Til and the Metaphysics of Postmodernism," *Reformed Perspectives Magazine* 6, 19 (2004), available at http://reformed perspectives.org/files/reformedperspectives/hall_of_frame/HOF.Hale.Derrida%20 and%20VanTil.6.30.04.html (accessed January 16, 2016).

Derrida would be the purest philosophical form of existential ethics" (*DG*, 188). Frame's description of existential ethics does accord with Derrida when he says that "ethical behavior, on this view, is not motivated by external reward, which would be mercenary, or by mere law, which would be drudgery" (*DG*, 187–88). The motivation of external reward is rejected by Derrida in his condemnation of reciprocal gift-giving or conditional hospitality, and his treatment of justice in "Force of Law" dismisses it as merely the following of rules. However, Frame mistakenly argues, at least with respect to Derrida, that existential ethics "adopts the view that ethics is essentially a matter of human inwardness, a matter of character and motive" (*DG*, 187), and that "there is no standard outside ourselves; what values there are in this world are the results of our decisions" (*DG*, 188). This description erroneously portrays Derrida as a subjectivist, whose ethics is governed by factors internal to the individual. This does not accord with Derrida's ethics, which, as we have seen, is about responding to the absolute injunction of the other and being open to the otherness to come, rather than being true to one's own inwardness. For Derrida, the only standard that matters is radically outside ourselves. If we content ourselves with our own standard, we will surely do great violence to alterity and singularity, and we will be closed to the injunction of the other. Furthermore, our own character and motives are what we, like Abraham, must lay aside in order to be open to the monstrous other.

The confusion, I think, comes in part from conflating a denial of objective truth with a denial of determinate truth. The absolute injunction of the other, and therefore the ethical responsibility with which I am faced, is, for Derrida, not a subjective feeling. There is a real other who places real demands on me. In this sense, the ethical demand is objective, though Derrida prefers to call it "absolute." What he denies is not the objectivity of this demand, but its predictability. The absolute demand of the other does not fit within the horizon of my expectation, and if I assume that it does, then it is no longer the demand of the other, but rather a predictable playing out · of my own expectations. So Derrida is not arguing that "there is no standard outside ourselves," but that there is no determinate standard outside ourselves that we can predict beforehand with absolute certainty. For Derrida, such a predictable standard would not really be outside ourselves at all, because it would always already have conformed to our (subjective) expectations. In order to be truly outside ourselves, a standard must exceed and confound our ability to predict it.

Once more in relation to Derrida's ethics, Frame argues both in *Apologetics: A Justification of Christian Belief* and in *Cornelius Van Til: An Analysis of His Thought* that deconstruction along with postmodernism more broadly "relativize all moral discourse while seeking to require everybody to conform to their values" (*CVT*, 84). We have already seen above that Derrida's ethics is based, not on a general relativism, but on the absoluteness of incommensurable values (for example, the relative values to me of my wife and my son), which cannot be calculated against each other. What is useful to point out in relation to Frame's claim, however, is the distinction between two different ideas of ethics which, in the literature on Derrida, often get labelled "morality" and "ethics" (or even "ethicity"). "Morality" is taken to mean a series of fixed and determinate laws or rules that seek to regulate behavior. To be moral is to obey a codified set of instructions without reflecting on the appropriateness or justice of doing so; it is to be "just following orders" and, to use the language of "Force of Law," it remains within the calculability of law (*droit*) and is therefore not just. Derrida does indeed reject such morality, not by relativizing it, but by deconstructing its "mystical foundation of authority." "Ethics," by contrast, stands before the absolute injunction of the other and asks, each time it has to make a decision or judgment in response to the other, whether the laws or rules that have been hitherto instituted are indeed just or not. It passes through the undecidability or aporia of the decision discussed above, and in each decision that it makes it affirms the law afresh, as if no rules previously existed, or it decides that the present law is not just.

In an illuminating passage from "Passions: 'An Oblique Offering,'" Derrida rejects both the claim that deconstruction is immoral and has no ethics, and the claim that it has a "morality" in the sense just described. If he had to choose between these two unsavory options, he would find "the remoralization of deconstruction" more appealing than its opposite, though both are distasteful to him. What Derrida seeks is not a system of morality, but an understanding of what it is about any system that makes it moral or ethical:

> What is the ethicity of ethics? The morality of morality? What is responsibility? What is the "What is?" in this case? etc. These questions are always urgent. In a certain way they must remain urgent and unanswered, at any rate without a general and rule-governed response, without a response other than that which is linked specifically each time, to the occurrence of a decision without rules and without will in the course of a new test of the undecidable. (*OTN*, 16–17)

We can see in this characterization of Derrida's ethical concerns a position very close to the "messianicity without messianism" discussed above. Derrida wants to keep the structure or the "ethicity" of ethics without signing up for a determinate ethical content that would deafen him to the arrival of any future monstrous other. Is Derrida here "seeking to require everybody to conform to [his] values," as Frame puts it? Not directly and in so many words, but he does not shrink from implying that

an openness to the other-to-come and a refusal to take any
determinate moral code as absolute are good for everyone. So
with the caveat that Derrida is not espousing a particular set of
determinate values, Frame is right insofar as an insistence upon
openness to the other-to-come presents itself as one particular
ethics among others and commends itself as better than other
positions.

In *The Doctrine of the Christian Life*, Frame groups Derrida
together with Lyotard, Lacan, Barthes, Foucault, and Rorty as
"the postmodern school," which is about as helpful as grouping Jean Calvin, the pope, the patriarch of Constantinople, Joel
Osteen, and Don Cupitt together as "the Christian school."
For these thinkers, he argues, "when we ask for the meaning
of a word, we get, as a definition, other words. So words refer
to other words, not to any objective reality" (*DCL*, 88). In
Derrida's case, this is half correct. When we ask for the meaning
of a word we do, as a matter of fact, get other words. This much
is uncontroversial and can be verified by moderns, postmoderns,
and amoderns alike when they open a dictionary. But it is not
quite right to say that Derrida is denying that words refer to a
nonlinguistic reality. Let's have a look at what Derrida says:

> It is totally false to suggest that deconstruction is a suspen-
> sion of reference. Deconstruction is always deeply concerned
> with the "other" of language. I never cease to be surprised by
> critics who see my work as a declaration that there is nothing
> beyond language; it is, in fact, saying the exact opposite. The
> critique of logocentrism is above all else the search for the
> "other" and the "other of language." (*DCP*, 154)

In what way do Frame and Derrida have their wires crossed here?
I think it is that when Frame evokes "objective reality," he assumes
this to mean a reality with determinate content, a reality that is

presented to us together with concepts and meanings such that, to use the example from Saussure discussed above, there really are rivers and streams out there in the world. By contrast, when Derrida insists that "deconstruction is always deeply concerned with the 'other' of language," he does not understand that other to be laden with conceptual meaning before the advent of the differing and deferring of différance. When Derrida searches for the other of language, he finds not a world full of determinate content and concepts (because all concepts always already participate in the differential play of meaning and are, in that sense, "inside the text"), but an absolute other that cannot be captured and presented within the iterable categories of language.

For Derrida, the other of language is not presentable within the economy of signs and meanings, laws, rules, and codes, of which language is a part. If it were, it would not be the other of language. To reconstruct Derrida's reasoning here, if language referred to something outside itself that could be adequately presented in language, then it would not really refer to something other than language at all. If language is to refer to something that is truly outside language, then it cannot do so by bringing that thing within language.

In the same section on postmodernism in *The Doctrine of the Christian Life*, Frame argues that "the task of the philosopher is 'deconstruction': to break down the connections that people think they are making between language and reality" (*DCL*, 89). This is a view echoed by William Edgar, who, in his introduction to Van Til's *Christian Apologetics*, states that "in some of the more extreme versions of postmodernism, such as deconstruction, language has no valid connection to reality."[4] Now it is true that the term "deconstruction" has gained a broad, nontechnical sense

---

4. William Edgar, introduction to *Christian Apologetics*, by Cornelius Van Til (Phillipsburg, NJ: P&R Publishing, 2003), 9.

today, such that it is often used as a synonym for "analysis" or even "destruction." Nevertheless, it is potentially misleading for Frame, in a section that mentions Derrida by name, to define deconstruction in the way he does. Deconstruction, as Derrida uses the term, does not break down the connections between language and reality, but stubbornly insists upon those connections, refusing that otherness and singularity be reduced to our (subjective, preconceived, prejudicial, iterable) categories, but letting the otherness of reality stand beyond and in opposition to our neat concepts. Deconstruction could be defined as a perpetual and irreducible demand that our language strive to do justice to the otherness of reality.

Frame also argues that "the views of postmodernists on these topics are rarely argued; they are merely presupposed. The post-modern conception of language rules out patient and careful argumentation about such topics, for every argument is a piece of language demanding deconstruction" (*DCL*, 89). This goes flatly against what Derrida is claiming for his own engagement with texts. Take, for instance, his description of his reading of Heidegger:

> Deconstruction moves, or makes its gestures, lines and divisions move, not only within the corpus [of a writer] in general, but at times within a single sentence, or a microscopic element of a corpus. Deconstruction mistrusts proper names: it will not say 'Heidegger in general' says thus or so; it will deal, in the micrology of the Heideggerian text, with different moments, different applications, concurrent logics, while trusting no generality and no configuration that is solid and given. It is a sort of great earthquake, a general tremor, which nothing can calm. I cannot treat a corpus, or a book, as a whole, and even the simple statement is subject to fission. (*TS*, 9)

Again, it appears to me that Frame and Derrida have their wires crossed in that they mean different things by being patient and careful here. Frame means logically and systematically presenting an argument with valid premises and a sound conclusion, whether or not the argument is formally set out as such. Derrida means a close and painstaking, even microscopic, reading of a text (his discussion of Rousseau's "Pronunciation" in *Of Grammatology* would be a good example) that brings out its internal tensions and inconsistencies. Derrida does not "merely presuppose" his arguments, but neither does he present them in a traditional way. His conception of language demands "patient and careful argumentation" precisely because the texts that form the basis of his arguments are always already deconstructing themselves.

In *A History of Western Philosophy and Theology*, Frame discusses Derrida, again alongside other contemporary writers, in a section entitled "Twentieth-Century Language Philosophy," which comes directly after a section on Saussure, whom Frame in this book considers Derrida's most significant influence. He characterizes Derrida's reading of Saussure by saying that "Jacques Derrida (1930–2004) pointed out that for Saussure, the meaning of every sign involves every other. So no meaning is ever fully available to us" (*HWPT*, 503), where "fully available to us" means, in words closer to Derrida's own language, fully present and self-identical, existing according to the metaphysics of presence and not according to différance. Frame is correct here. He is once again on the money when he says that deconstruction is "opposed to the idea of absolute certainty" (*HWPT*, 584).

Nevertheless, Frame goes on to confuse Derrida with Roland Barthes's idea of the "death of the author" when he affirms that "contrary to deconstructionists . . . he [Kevin Vanhoozer] argues that the intention of a text's author does indeed carry weight in its interpretation" (*HWPT*, 546). This is once more a common confusion, and so it is worth trying to clear it up. It is certainly true that Derrida often reads texts against what appear to be the author's own arguments, but in order to do so, he must first reconstruct and understand what those arguments are. In *Of Grammatology*, he calls the sort of reading that simply affirms what the author is taken to have meant a "doubling commentary," and he is far from dismissive of such reading:

> This moment of doubling commentary should no doubt have its place in a critical reading. To recognize and respect all its classical exigencies is not easy and requires all the instruments of traditional criticism. Without this recognition and this respect, critical production would risk developing in any direction at all and authorize itself to say almost anything. (*OG*, 158)

So the author's intended meaning does indeed "carry weight" for Derrida in the interpretation of the text, but it does not have the final word. Derrida shows (and again his reading of Rousseau in *Of Grammatology* is a good example of this) how texts run away from their authors like faulty shopping carts in the supermarket, thwarting the author's intention by veering off in unintended directions, by contradicting themselves or by in fact suggesting the opposite of what the author thought he was saying. As for Barthes's idea itself, Derrida dismisses "that death or omission of the author of which, as is certainly the case, too much of a case has been made" (*S*, 22).

Derrida's Style and Van Tilian "Epistemological Self-Consciousness"

Having dealt in the previous section with a number of misunderstandings that haunt the reception of Derrida's work, both in Reformed circles and wider afield, I feel the need to deal with one more Derridean stumbling block before launching into a Van Tilian reading proper. It is the matter of Derrida's style. Most new readers of Derrida's texts (and many seasoned ones too!) find themselves frustrated or disorientated by the way in which Derrida writes. He is not easy to read, and many commentators have held this against him in no uncertain terms, accusing him of deliberate obscurantism and saying that his body of work is incoherent charlatanism. One of the most famous examples is an article by the speech act philosopher John Searle in the *New York Review of Books* in 1984:

> Anyone who reads deconstructive texts with an open mind is likely to be struck by the same phenomena that initially surprised me: the low level of philosophical argumentation, the deliberate obscurantism of the prose, the wildly exaggerated claims, and the constant striving to give the appearance of profundity by making claims that seem paradoxical, but under analysis often turn out to be silly or trivial. (*LI*, 25–26)

In addressing the legitimate question that Searle raises about Derrida's writing, I will restrict myself to highlighting the facet of Derrida's style that is most relevant, I think, for Reformed readers, and one that is often missed. It is this: the way in which Derrida writes shows the importance that he places on epistemological self-consciousness, which is also given high value in Van Tilian thought.

What does it mean to be epistemologically self-conscious? It means that we should be aware of our epistemological position (what we think it is possible to know, and how we can know it), rather than just falling into this or that epistemological position without even being aware of having done so. It also means that our metaphysics (what we think exists) should not overreach this epistemology, claiming things that—by our own account—we cannot possibly know. For example, Van Til argues, the Christian has good reason to affirm the orderliness and regularity of the world, because she understands that regularity to have its origin and ground in God's character. An epistemologically self-conscious nonbeliever, such as David Hume, will refrain from making any absolute claims about the objective orderliness of the universe because he knows that he has no basis for such claims: every time he has seen one billiard ball strike another so far in his life, the second has started moving, but that is no guarantee that the balls will do the same the next time he looks or that the movement of the balls reveals to him a universal law of causality. By contrast, the epistemologically unself-conscious nonbeliever will make epistemological claims for which his metaphysical system gives him no ontological warrant (one such claim would be dogmatic atheism: that we can know for certain that there is no God), writing epistemological checks that his ontology cannot cash. Van Til, indeed, argues that all epistemological claims resting on a materialistic view of the world are unfounded:

> Suppose we think of a man made of water in an infinitely extended and bottomless ocean of water. Desiring to get out of water, he makes a ladder of water. He sets this ladder upon the water and against the water and then attempts to climb out of the water. So hopeless and senseless a picture must be drawn of the natural man's methodology based as it is upon the assumption that time or chance is ultimate. On his assumption his own rationality is a product of chance. On his assumption even the laws of logic which he employs are products of chance. The rationality and purpose that he may be searching for are still bound to be products of chance. (*DF*, 124–25)

One aspect of what we might call "epistemological insouciance" (the opposite of epistemological self-consciousness) is that it is possible to undermine the content of what one says by how one says it. Let's start with a simple example. If I say, "I am unable to speak," then, without further clarification, my hearer would be within her rights to suggest that what I have just said seems to be undermined by the very fact that I have said it. If I cannot speak, how can I say, "I cannot speak"?

Moving a little closer to Derrida, if one's philosophical intention is to show that language is not a transparent mirror through which we see a stable world, but a system of shifting differences that provide us with the concepts that make up that "world," and within and between which meaning is always differing and deferred, then it does little to help the reader get a feel for this condition of existence if one writes crystalline, limpid, transparent prose. Such prose itself could, of course, be deconstructed, but this would not be obvious to the reader not already familiar with deconstruction. So I think it can reasonably be argued that Derrida is emphasizing—and, yes, sometimes exaggerating—the opacity of language itself, the fact that it is not a neutral window onto an extra-textual reality, but the thread out of which the shifting fabric of our apprehension of that reality is woven, and that he is doing this to try to help the reader see what he is saying.

Three examples of this will suffice, I hope, to give a rough sense of how Derrida seeks to achieve this end. The first example shows how he uses language in ways that make linguistic ambiguity visible, showing that its meaning is not unitary and settled. One of the best-known examples of this is a short phrase with which we are already familiar: "tout autre est tout autre" (usually translated "every other is wholly other"). Taking out the middle copula, both parts of this phrase are lexically identical, but they occur within the context of Derrida's meditation on Kierkegaard to mean different things: first "every other" and then "wholly other." Another instance of exploiting double meanings in this way would be Derrida's essay on the French philosopher Maurice Blanchot entitled *Pas*, a word which in French can mean both "step" and "not," evoking both movement and stasis at once.

The second example of Derrida's style is his repetition of nearly synonymous homonymous or homophonous words, often placing two, sometimes three such verbs or nouns next to each other in order that the reader can reflect on the nuances and differences that each term brings to what Derrida is saying. Examples of this can be found in almost every page of Derrida's writing. Opening *Limited Inc* at random, I see near synonyms in the sentence "Fiction can always *re-work, remark* every other type of iteration" (*LI*, 100; emphasis mine), and in the course of responding to John Searle's *Reply* to his previous essay "Signature Event Context," Derrida writes, "In *reiterating* what can be read on each page of *SEC*, *re-plying* or *reapplying* it, it is difficult to see how the *Reply* can object to it" (*LI*, 47; emphasis mine). One effect of repeating such near synonyms, homonyms, and homophones is to make language visible, to remind us that words are not a transparent window through which we see the world, but have their own fabric and texture. It also reminds us that there is more than one possible way of expressing a given idea and also that the mode of expression is inseparable from the idea itself: if something is said differently, something different is said.

The third and final example is Derrida's tendency to talk about what he says as he says it, or to reflect on his own language. Here is a translation of the opening words from "The Law of Genre," an address given at a conference in Strasbourg in 1979:

> No mixing of genres.
> I will not mix genres.
> I repeat: no mixing of genres. I will not mix them.

Now suppose I let these utterances resonate all by themselves. Suppose: I abandon them to their fate, I set free their random virtualities and turn them over to your hearing, to whatever mobility they retain and you bestow upon them to engender effects of all kinds without my having to stand behind them.

I merely said, and then repeated: no mixing of genres; I will not mix them.

As long as I release these utterances (which others might call speech acts) in a form yet scarcely determined, given the open context out of which I have just let them be grasped from "my" language—as long as I do this, you may find it difficult to choose among several interpretative options. They are legion, as I could demonstrate. (*AL*, 223)

Some readers of Derrida have taken textual features such as these as a reason to write him off as a serious thinker, and of course they are free to do so—although in my opinion the decision is hasty. In the spirit of *audi alteram partem* ("listen to the other side"), we can see these features of Derrida's style as, at least in part, attempts at (1) epistemological self-consciousness, (2) showing the reader the condition of language and meaning that he describes, rather than just telling her about it, and (3) helping her to feel its force—and its frustration—rather than just describing it. His texts are, in his own words, "performative performances" (*TS*, 65).

5

DERRIDA AND VAN TIL IN THE LIGHT OF JOHN 1:1–18

Rather than organizing the rest of this book as a structural repetition of its first half, with sections on metaphysics, ethics/politics, and theology, I have chosen to elaborate a Van Tilian response to Derrida by discussing the prologue to John's gospel, with occasional references to Colossians 1. I hope that this will allow the Bible to speak for itself and on its own terms, just as it was my intention in the first half of this book to let Derrida set the agenda and speak in his own terms. It will also ensure that the argument remains close to the text of the Bible, an idea which both Derridean close reading and Reformed theology would welcome. Other passages could no doubt have been chosen, and there are other things that one could say from the Bible in response to Derrida's thought that are not mentioned in these passages (as indeed there were many aspects of Derrida's thought that were not covered in the first half of the book). Nevertheless, I hope this particular approach will facilitate a conversation between Derrida's texts and the Bible that allows both to come with their own assumptions and concepts and allows us to gain a Reformed perspective on the broad movements and commitments of Derrida's thought, rather than just dealing with this or that isolated idea or statement.

Here is the passage in full, with verse numbers included and the parts to which I will pay specific attention italicized:

> In the beginning was the Word, and the Word was with God, and the Word was God. [2] He was in the beginning with God. [3] All things were made through him, and without him was not any thing made that was made. [4] In him was life, and the life was the light of men. [5] The light shines in the darkness, and the darkness has not overcome it.
>
> [6] There was a man sent from God, whose name was John. [7] He came as a witness, to bear witness about the light, that all might believe through him. [8] He was not the light, but came to bear witness about the light.
>
> [9] The true light, which gives light to everyone, was coming into the world. [10] He was in the world, and the world was made through him, yet the world did not know him. [11] He came to his own, and his own people did not receive him. [12] But to all who did receive him, who believed in his name, *he gave the right to become children of God,* [13] who were born, *not of blood nor of the will of the flesh nor of the will of man,* but of God.
>
> [14] And *the Word became flesh and dwelt among us,* and we have seen his glory, glory as of the only Son from the Father, full of grace and truth. [15] (John bore witness about him, and cried out, "This was he of whom I said, 'He who comes after me ranks before me, because he was before me.'") [16] For *from his fullness we have all received, grace upon grace.* [17] For the law was given through Moses; grace and truth came through Jesus Christ. [18] No one has ever seen God; *the only God, who is at the Father's side, he has made him known.*

The Creator-Creature Distinction and
"There Is Nothing Outside the Text"

Above I showed that, for Derrida, everything that exists (everything that "there is") exists in the same way: "différantly." But John 1 introduces us to two very different modes of being. First there is "the Word," who was "in the beginning" (v. 1) and who made everything "that was made" (not everything "that exists," for God exists, but was not made) (v. 3). Then, of course, there is the second mode of being, that of "all things" that were made through the Word (v. 3). Right off the bat, this gives biblical Christianity a very different understanding of "all things" than that of Derrida, for whom there is only one mode of being. The difference between the two modes of being in John 1 is expressed by Cornelius Van Til's famous two circles and what has come to be known as "the Creator-creature distinction." This understanding of reality, at its most basic level, affirms that there is one fundamental ontological division: between God and everything else. Van Til explains:

> I point out that the Bible does contain a theory of Reality. And this theory of Reality is that of two levels of being, first, of God as infinite, eternal, and unchangeable and, second, of the universe as derivative, finite, temporal, and changeable. A position is best known by its most basic differentiation. The meanings of all words in the Christian theory of being depend upon the differentiation between the self-contained God and the created universe. (*DF*, 237)

One important aspect of the Creator-creature distinction that Van Til draws out is that Creator and creation do not "exist" in the same way. God's existence is "infinite, eternal, and unchangeable," but the creation exists as "derivative, finite, temporal, and changeable." A biblical understanding of reality has to reckon with two very different modes of being. In fact, Van Til erects the Creator-creature distinction as fundamental to all biblical thinking, criticizing any apologist who does not "make the Creator-creature distinction basic in all that he says about anything."[1] But doesn't Derrida also posit something like Van Til's duality of modes of being when he speaks of the "impossible," or of justice, "if there is such a thing"? In other words, isn't the absolute otherness that cannot be articulated in iterable language, before which I am responsible and to which all my discourse and action seeks to do justice, a functional equivalent of God? No, it is not, and neither Derrida nor Van Til would be happy with the claim that it is. For a start, Derrida's justice is impossible precisely because it is not a mode of being at all. Justice does not exist in the sense of being able to be presented to us in a particular code or judgment. It is not transcendent, existing in some realm separate from our everyday experience. So what is it? Justice is for Derrida a demand, from the other, to do better when it comes to speaking of the singular in iterable language: "For in the end, where would deconstruction find its force, its movement or its motivation if not in this always unsatisfied appeal, beyond the given determinations of what one names, in determined contexts, justice, the possibility of justice?" (*AR*, 249). Derridean justice, furthermore, cannot be identified with any positive description, whereas, as we shall see, the God of John 1 reveals himself in particular, determinate ways. For these reasons, Derrida's justice (or gift, or hospitality) is not Van Til's Creator.

---

1. The phrase appears in the electronic version of the first edition of *Defense of the Faith,* but not in the fourth edition. The sentiment is repeated often in Van Til's other writings.

One consequence of the lack of a Creator-creature distinction in Derrida's thought is that God's power is treated as if it were just like a human being monopolizing power for himself: as dangerous and violent. If there is only one sort of being, and if an accumulation of power in the hands of one human being is a dangerous thing, then there is no qualitative difference between human despotism and divine sovereignty. Derrida's thought has the great virtue of ensuring that we do not think more highly of ourselves than we ought, in terms of our epistemic capacities or our claims to be just. But in being so anxious that we do not think too much of ourselves, his thought does not allow us to think highly enough of God. In order to undermine human pretensions to sovereign power without a Creator-creature distinction, it is necessary to have a powerless God. I will come back to the "despot" argument when I discuss the relation of the biblical God to Derrida's distinction between law and justice.

The Creator-creature distinction does lead Reformed thinking to something not unlike Derrida's affirmation that "there is nothing outside the text." Both Derrida and the Van Tilian tradition of thought reject the idea of pure, unmediated access to knowledge, free of all context. Furthermore, neither position sees this as a drawback, but rather as a guard against hubris. We have seen that, for Derrida, a claim to speak in definitive terms about a singular entity is to do violence to it. In a similar way, John Frame argues that the fact that every position is situated is not an embarrassment to Reformed theology, but a guard against idolatry:

> Sometimes we dream fondly of a "purely objective" knowledge of God—a knowledge of God freed from the limitations of our senses, minds, experiences, preparation, and so forth. . . . A "purely objective" knowledge is precisely what we

don't want! Such knowledge would presuppose a denial of
our creaturehood and thus a denial of God and of all truth.
(*DKG*, 65)

The situated nature of all human knowledge is a consequence
of the Creator-creature distinction: only God is above creation,
and every perspective within creation is limited and situated.
This is not a defect, but the condition of being a creature. The
assertion that it is biblical to understand all human knowledge
as situated requires a little further explanation, however, for it is
easily misunderstood to sanction a simplistic cultural relativism.
In order better to grasp the nuanced biblical understanding of
the situatedness of knowledge, let us briefly consider the song
of the great multitude in Revelation 7:

> After this I looked, and behold, a great multitude that no one
> could number, from every nation, from all tribes and peoples
> and languages, standing before the throne and before the
> Lamb, clothed in white robes, with palm branches in their
> hands, and crying out with a loud voice, "Salvation belongs
> to our God who sits on the throne, and to the Lamb!" (Rev.
> 7:9–10)

We can make three observations about the situatedness of
knowledge from this passage. First, biblical truth is not acultural. Even in the new heavens and the new earth, the worship
of God is not (and should not be) abstracted from specific
cultural identities and forms. Revelation does not present us
with some abstract, universal Esperanto of worship, nor are
those gathered in this passage presented in a culturally neutral way. Christian cultural critic Lesslie Newbigin helpfully
notes that "the idea that one can or could at any time separate
out by some process of distillation a pure gospel unadulterated

by any cultural accretions is an illusion."[2] This is not merely incidental, Newbigin insists. To suggest that the gospel can be understood or communicated apart from any culture is "an abandonment of the gospel, for the gospel is about the Word made flesh."[3] So the gospel is always situated.

Secondly, it is equally important to stress that biblical truth is not monocultural. There is no culture that is better suited than all the others to receive the gospel message, such that as Christians mature they will all gravitate toward that one culture. On the contrary, the worship of the new earth gathers people from every tongue, tribe, and nation. As Newbigin once more argues, the biblical gospel "must therefore call into question every human culture."[4] Thirdly, a helpful way to describe the biblical understanding of situated knowledge is to say that it is "transcultural." The message of the Bible and the ability to sing God's praises are not confined to any one culture; rather, members of all tongues, tribes, and nations can equally praise God around his throne in heaven without having to leave their tongues or their nations at the door. Each culture remains situated, and the message of the Bible will affirm some aspects of all cultures and challenge some aspects of all cultures. It can find a home in all cultures as it transforms each of them from within. The Bible neither validates any culture just as it is (a monocultural gospel) nor rejects any culture out of hand (an acultural gospel). As Miroslav Volf puts it, "Religion must be de-ethnicized so that ethnicity can be de-sacralized."[5]

2. Lesslie Newbigin, *Foolishness to the Greeks: The Gospel and Western Culture* (Grand Rapids: Eerdmans, 1986), 4.

3. Ibid., 4.

4. Ibid., 3–4.

5. Miroslav Volf, *Exclusion and Embrace: A Theological Exploration of Identity, Otherness, and Reconciliation* (Nashville: Abingdon Press, 1996), 49.

Absolute Personality Theism
and Ontotheology

We have already begun, in our discussion of the Creator-creature distinction, to explore what it means for God to be "absolute." God is absolute in that he is not a part of his creation (not part of all "that was made") and not mixed in with creation (though we shall see in our discussion of Colossians 1 that he is intimately involved with it at all moments and in all its parts). As well as being absolute, however, the God of John 1 is personal. As John's prologue continues, it becomes clear that the "Word" (*logos*) of which John is speaking is not an "it" but a "he." This *logos* is on the Creator side of the Creator-creature distinction in verse 1. We learn that he was "the light of men" (v. 4) and that this light was "in the world" (v. 10), "came to his own" (v. 11), and "became flesh and dwelt among us" (v. 14). Finally, in verse 17, he is given the name "Jesus Christ." In his first eighteen verses, John makes ineluctably clear that the absolute Creator is a person—not just "personal" or "personhood" as an abstract concept, but a specific person: Jesus Christ.

John Frame has helpfully given this biblical picture of God the title "absolute personality theism":

> The major religions of the world, in their most typical (one tends to say "authentic") forms, are either pantheistic (Hinduism, Taoism) or polytheistic (animism, some forms of Hinduism, Shinto, and the traditional religions of Greece, Rome, Egypt, etc.). Pantheism has an absolute, but not a personal absolute. Polytheism has personal gods, but none of these is absolute. Indeed, although most religions tend to emphasize either pantheistic absolutism or personal nonabsolutism, we can usually find both elements beneath the surface. In Greek polytheism, for example, the gods are

personal but not absolute. However, this polytheism is sup-
plemented by a doctrine of fate, which is a kind of impersonal
absolute. Similarly, behind the gods of animism is Mana, the
impersonal reality. People seem to have a need or a desire
for both personality and absoluteness, but in most religions
these two elements are separated and therefore compromise
one another, rather than reinforcing one another. Thus, of
the major religious movements, only biblical religion calls us
with clarity to worship a personal absolute. (*AGG*, 38–39)

It is important to grasp just how radical this personalism has
been taken to be in recent Reformed thought. Nothing is more
absolute than the personal God. Logic is reliant on God, not
determinate of him, for:

> There were no principles of truth, goodness, or beauty that
> were next to or above God according to which he patterned
> the world. The principles of truth, goodness, and beauty are
> to be thought of as identical with God's being; they are the
> attributes of God. (*DF*, 10)

In the universe as described by the Bible, there is nothing
more original, more simple, or more fundamental than God
and his character. He is not the product of logic; rather, the law
of noncontradiction itself is "the expression on a created level
of the internal coherence of God's nature" (*IST*, 11). Logic is
the product of God's character and part of its expression in creation. There is nothing before, behind, or underneath God upon
which he relies, nothing simpler or more primordial than God
(not matter, not energy, not universal laws, not mathematics)
to which he can be reduced. We live in a universe, the ultimate
and most fundamental explanation and ground of which is the
absolute personality of God. This also entails that, while logic

is not fundamental, it is not arbitrary either. If there is to be a creation, then it will be one of order and logic (and of much else besides), reflecting God's character. God "cannot deny himself" (2 Tim. 2:13), and his character dictates, so to speak, how he will act and how he will create.

One further concomitant of absolute personality theism is that, as Van Til puts it in his *Introduction to Systematic Theology*, when God revealed himself to us, "there was no universal being of which he was a particular instance" (*IST*, 232). God is not subordinate to, or less fundamental than, "being," any more than he is subordinate to, or less fundamental than, logic. Everything that exists in creation began to exist and continues to exist because God has willed it, including order and logic, and his own existence is not one instance of a fundamental reality that we could call "being," but is itself original and fundamental.

This presents a very different picture from the ontotheology that Derrida rejects, which describes an impersonal, uncaused cause that sets the universe in motion and is defined as "pure thought" or "thought thinking itself." In recent decades and centuries, this "god of the philosophers" has been associated with the mathematizing philosophy of rationalists like Descartes, who inform much of the "modernism" that many "postmoderns" are quick to reject. Indeed, Derrida's critique of ontotheology and of a mathematizable modernist view of the world is valuable to Reformed thinkers to the extent that Christianity remains in thrall to modernist ways of thinking, with its assumption that we can have direct epistemological access to a neutral, objective reality, and that reality is transparent to language. A note of caution needs to be sounded, however. Some "postmodern" Christians give the impression that the whole of Christianity is exclusively and thoroughly modern, and that the only possible solution is to make it all thoroughly postmodern. Finding the frying pan a little hot, they suggest we relocate to the fire.

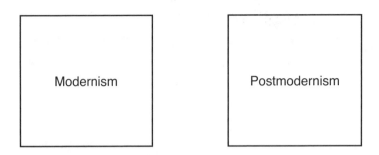

Fig. 5.1. The False Dichotomy between Modernism and Postmodernism

The value of absolute personality theism in this debate is that it cuts across the modernist/postmodernist dilemma. If the reader will allow a neologism that, I hope, will prove useful as we move through this Reformed reading of Derrida, absolute personality theism "diagonalizes" the modernism/postmodernism debate, which is to say that it falls into neither of the categories on offer, but does not utterly reject them, either, while showing them both to be inadequate. So how does absolute personality theism diagonalize the modern/postmodern dichotomy? It shows that modernism and postmodernism share the fundamental assumption that the bedrock reality of the universe, whatever it be, is impersonal. The difference between personalism and impersonalism is, as we shall see again and again below, so fundamental that, when faced with biblical personalism, modernism and postmodernism look like subtle variations on a theme, rather than the chalk and cheese that advocates of postmodern Christianity seem to think they are.

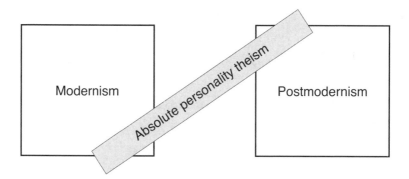

Fig. 5.2. Absolute Personality Theism Diagonalizes the False Dichotomy between Modernism and Postmodernism

It would be a valuable exercise to critique the ways in which contemporary Christian thought has departed from the Bible in aping the dominant modernist thought-forms of the last three hundred or so years. There are, however, two possible ways of undertaking such an exercise. The first would be to critique all the things Christians say that happen to coincide with what modernists also say. But that would be unhelpful. It would hardly be more sensible than rejecting every sentence we might utter that is the same as one spoken by Adolf Hitler (even if it is something like "I would like a cup of tea" or "good morning"), for no other reason than that Adolf Hitler once said it. The second— and more sensible—way to critique Christianity's modernism would be to highlight all those points at which contemporary Christianity sides with modern philosophy against the biblical witness, not because of its agreement with modernism at those points, but because of its disagreement with the Bible. The deconstruction of modernist assumptions offered by Derrida can be very helpful to this second sort of critique, because it shines a light into the dark corners of our thought and exposes our assumptions. What is more, this second sort of critique is at the heart of the constant vigilance of a reforming Christianity

under the banner of *semper reformanda* ("always reforming").
The battle is not against modernism, nor against postmodernism, but rather against those moments in both ways of thinking that clearly depart from a biblical pattern—granted that it is
not always easy to understand precisely what that pattern is, or
whether and to what extent a particular philosophical position
departs from it.

Absolute personality is also crucial in diagonalizing Derrida's
dichotomy of law and justice. Derrida, it will be remembered,
makes a distinction between law (*droit*) and justice (*justice*),
where the former is a codified, calculable set of rules to which
one can adhere mindlessly, and the latter, "if there is such a
thing," is absolute and cannot be captured and presented, such
that one could ever say with certainty, "I know that I am just."
But the biblical idea of law conforms to neither of these options,
because it arises within the context—and within the creation—
of the absolutely personal God. Consider the archetypal expression of law in the Bible: the Ten Commandments. The passage
begins in the following way:

> And God spoke all these words, saying,
> "I am the LORD your God, who brought you out of the
> land of Egypt, out of the house of slavery.
> "You shall have no other gods before me.
> "You shall not make for yourself a carved image, or any
> likeness of anything that is in heaven above, or that is in the
> earth beneath, or that is in the water under the earth." (Ex.
> 20:1–4)

The commandments here are framed, not as a procedural code,
but as, first, an expression of Yahweh's character. He presents
himself, not as a universal truth or objective principle, but as
a person (with a proper name) who is active in history: "the

LORD your God, who brought you out of the land of Egypt." Secondly, the commandments are given, as the first verse points out, after God's rescue of his covenant people from Egypt, at the point where they are setting up a new society in the desert under his rule. In other words, there is an irreducible relational and redemptive context to the commands. Putting these two points together, we conclude that the commandments cannot be separated from the God whose character they express, and they cannot be separated from the fact that God's people have been rescued to have a new relationship with him. This cannot be reduced to Derrida's law (*droit*), and it has much more content than his justice.

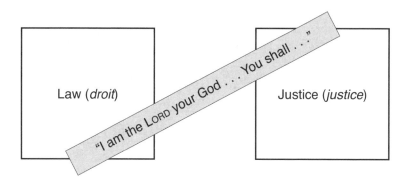

Fig. 5.3. Absolute Personality Theism Diagonalizes Calculating Law and Impossible Justice

Absolute personality theism as a foundation of God's commands resolves neither to unthinking, calculable, propositional content nor to an absolute, punctual, immediate demand from the other. Scripture provides a context of God's character and trustworthiness that situates the singular claims he might make on individuals. God commanded Abraham to sacrifice his son Isaac, but that command did not come in a contextual vacuum. Abraham knew enough of God, of his character and his faithfulness (we might say his personality), to obey not simply because the command was singular and came as an absolute injunction from the other, nor because it fitted a preestablished universal moral code (the two options Derrida considers), but because, in Paul's terms, Abraham knew the one whom he believed (2 Tim. 1:12):

> By faith Abraham, when he was tested, offered up Isaac, and *he who had received the promises* was in the act of offering up his only son, of whom it was said, "Through Isaac shall your offspring be named." *He considered that God was able even to raise him from the dead*, from which, figuratively speaking, he did receive him back. (Heb. 11:17–19)

To follow a rule or law is to "know that" (in this case, to know that people should not sacrifice their offspring); to heed a singular call is not to know that, but to obey in the face of the screaming prohibitions of morality. But the commandments of an absolutely personal God diagonalize this opposition: to obey the commands of Yahweh is to "know who."

Trinity, Différance, and "Every Other Is Wholly Other"

To say that the biblical God is absolute and personal is not yet enough, for the Bible also shows him to be a Trinity. The word *Trinity* is not in the Bible, of course, but neither is the word *person* to describe God, and neither, for that matter, is the word *Bible* itself, yet that does not prevent all these terms from being useful for summing up biblical teaching on a particular subject. John gestures toward the Trinity in his prologue by baldly juxtaposing two unqualified statements: the Word was "with God" (and therefore distinct from God), and the Word "was God" (and therefore identified with God). Trinitarianism is, along with the Creator-creature distinction and absolute personality, the third great pillar in a biblical view of reality that will allow us to find both similarities and differences with Derrida's thought.

Van Til frequently insists that biblical Trinitarianism provides a distinctively Christian response to the philosophical problem of the one and the many:

> Using the language of the One-and-Many question we contend that in God the one and the many are equally ultimate. Unity in God is no more fundamental than diversity, and diversity in God is no more fundamental than unity. The persons of the Trinity are mutually exhaustive of one another. The Son and the Spirit are ontologically on a par with the Father.[6]

This insistence upon equal ultimacy stands in contrast to some strands of Neoplatonic Christian thinking, according to which the abstract unity of God's essence is prioritized above Trinitarian multiplicity. If God is perfect, then he must be one in a deeper way than he is three. But this is not the biblical view: plurality is just as "perfect" as unity, and just as fundamental to who God is. The mistake to avoid here is to think that the Christian Trinity provides a "response" to the problem of the one and the many in the terms in which that problem is customarily stated. The problem, as handed down by Plato, is that of how to relate abstract unity to concrete plurality. (How can we say that all the "stones" in the world are all "stones"? Is that just a trick of language, or is there some essence of stone-ness shared by all stones and by no non-stones?) Is unity first, as Parmenides

---

6. Cornelius Van Til, *The Defense of the Faith* (Philadelphia: Presbyterian and Reformed, 1955), 26.

thought, or is plurality first, as Heraclitus suggests? As we have seen, absolute personality theism denies that abstraction (either abstract unity or abstract plurality) is ultimate: God is not a collection of fundamental abstract qualities, but a Trinity whose absolute character may be spoken of in terms of qualities. The Trinity does not, therefore, provide an answer to the problem of the one and the many as usually understood; it challenges the terms in which that problem is stated. In short, it diagonalizes the problem.

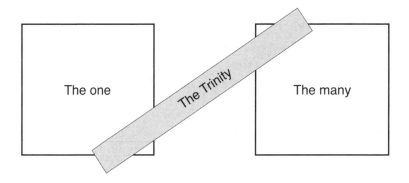

Fig. 5.4. The Trinity Diagonalizes the One and the Many

How does this Trinitarian "equal ultimacy" of the one and the many differ from a deconstructive understanding of the one and the many, which for Derrida would be better termed "identity" and "difference"? To begin with, within Derridean thought both identity and difference are constructed from the fundamental condition of differing and deferring that Derrida calls différance. Neither simple unity nor simple plurality is primary. Secondly, however, although différance and difference are not the same thing, Derrida nevertheless maintains an originary differing and deferring and not an originary identity (which would be the metaphysics of presence). He evokes "arche-writing" as the shared condition of both speech and writing, not "arche-speech."

By contrast, the unity and diversity in the Trinity are not effects of a shared condition of being that gives rise to them both (some "arche-personhood" that would give rise to both the "three persons" and the "one God" of the Trinity); rather, they are both equally ultimate. God's unity does not ground his diversity, and his diversity does not ground his unity. The thrust of a Trinitarian critique of différance is to assert the equal ultimacy of the one and of the many in God.

In this way, we could say that Derrida and ontotheology present us with a binary choice that Trinitarianism diagonalizes. Différance is the condition of possibility of both identity and difference for Derrida, and identity precedes difference for ontotheology. Biblical Christianity, however, refuses the claim that difference or identity is fundamentally derivative (both are derivative for Derrida; difference is derivative for ontotheology). "God is one God" and "God is three persons" do not vie with each other for supremacy. In biblical Christianity, there is an equality between unity and diversity, between identity and difference, that we do not find either in Derrida or in ontotheology. Derrida's critique of the origin is that there is no single, unitary, self-identical, and differentiated point of origin, but rather an origin that is always already different from itself and deferred in relation to itself. The Trinity splits the horns of this dilemma and gives a third option: an origin that incorporates both difference and unity without either of them compromising the other, and which, furthermore, introduces the notion of personality all the way down.

Can we say, then, that the Trinity "deconstructs" binary oppositions (like "one" and "many")? Not really, because, as we have seen, deconstruction discerns the differing and deferring of différance as the condition of possibility for all such oppositions, and there is no pre-Trinitarian différance: God's unity and his plurality are equally originary. One of the major differences here is that, for Derrida, originary identity and originary différance is a zero-sum game: to deconstruct the metaphysics of presence is not to leave it as it was thought to be, with its original identity and presence, but to show that identity and presence were never original at all. There is either an assumption of the metaphysics of presence or there is a demonstration of how that metaphysics deconstructs itself, but not both at the same time.

Moving, so to speak, from heaven to earth, Van Tilian thought takes it that the equal ultimacy of the one and the many in the ontological Trinity is a pattern for the relation of the one and the many within creation:

> As Christians, we hold that in this universe we deal with a derivative one and many, which can be brought into fruitful relation with one another because, back of both, we have in God the original One and Many. If we are to have coherence in our experience, there must be a correspondence of our experience to the eternally coherent experience of God. Human knowledge ultimately rests upon the internal coherence within the Godhead; our knowledge rests upon the ontological Trinity as its presupposition. (*IST*, 23)

One implication of this is that there is no necessity, within a Trinitarian frame, to play unity and diversity, identity and difference, or sameness and otherness off against each other. In terms of Derrida's thought, we have seen that "every other is wholly other," and that therefore to use iterable language to speak of singular entities always does violence to those entities. But is "every other is wholly other" in the Bible? Once more, the answer is not a straightforward one, but must be stated as a "yes, but." Every other is wholly other in absolute personality theism because each individual (human, animal, object) is uniquely created, known and loved by God, and cannot be substituted for any other. The parable of the shepherd who leaves his ninety-nine sheep to search for the one who is lost (Matt. 18:10–14), and Jesus's reassurance that "even the hairs of your head are all numbered" (Luke 12:7), affirm that each individual is uniquely loved.[7] In this sense, yes, every other is wholly other. However, every other is not wholly other in Derrida's sense that it is *a priori* violent to speak of it in iterable language. What biblical Trinitarianism leads us to expect in the world (perfectly in the world of the first creation and the final redeemed community of God's people, but imperfectly in this fallen world) is not radical singularity, heterogeneity, and resistance to categories, but a harmony of unity and diversity. John Frame explains:

> In God's world, everything is, after all, comparable to everything else. Granted, we tend to wince a bit when something we love or admire is compared to what we consider an unworthy object. But remember, Scripture even compares God to an unjust judge. Everything is related to everything else. There is nothing that "has nothing to do with" anything else. The strength of anti-abstractionism is that it recognizes that fact. (*DKG*, 231–32)

This is so because God's creation reflects his own co-ultimacy of unity and plurality, and also because all things have in common that they are created and sustained by God and will be brought under Christ. This commonality of all things is expressed succinctly in Paul's description in Colossians 1 of the cosmic role of Christ:

---

7. God's love for individuals also provides an absolute personality theistic response to the thorny philosophical problem of individuation: how we decide what constitutes "one" thing—or, to put it another way, the problem of where one thing stops and another thing starts.

> For by him all things were created, in heaven and on earth,
> visible and invisible, whether thrones or dominions or rulers
> or authorities—all things were created through him and for
> him. And he is before all things, and in him all things hold
> together. (Col. 1:16–17)

In this passage, we see once more the dovetailing of unity and
diversity. No less than four times Paul insists that he is talking
about "all things": all things have something in common, and
there is no exception. But those "all things" are still plural, and
not various manifestations or modes of one singular thing, as
they would be, for example, in pantheism. What "all things"
have in common is that they were all created by Christ, created
for him, and hold together in him. In other words, Christ (to
speak infelicitously for a moment) is the glue that holds an
otherwise atomized world together and makes it one world
rather than a collection of radically unrelated objects. For the
Christian, every other is not wholly other for the reason that
every other is from Christ, exists through him, and exists ulti-
mately for him. Within a Derridean frame, reducing absolute
alterity in this way opens the door to reducing the responsibility that we have before the other, but in the biblical view this
is not the case. In fact, because everything belongs to Christ
and is made to bring him glory, we are directly answerable
to him and responsible before him for the way in which we
treat even the smallest element of the world he has made. It is
not necessary for something to be radically and wholly other
to me for me to feel the force of my responsibility before it.
The absolute ethical injunction to deal with even the smallest
"things" of creation in a way that is "for Christ" comes from
their relation to him, not from their absolute transcendence
of my epistemological categories and my inability to fit them
within a prescribed frame of meaning.

Accommodation, Language, and Violence

We have already begun to see that the absolutely personal Trinitarian God of the Bible is far from the impersonal, unknowable, unitary, and self-contained Prime Mover of ontotheology. One of the most striking differences, and one which has profound implications for a Van Tilian reading of Derrida, is the incarnation of the second person of the Trinity. John, as many commentators have pointed out, is almost crude in bluntly stating that "the Word became flesh" (*logos sarx egeneto*), where *sarx* means "flesh" in the full sense of blood and bone. The great scandal of the verse, however, I would suggest, is in its verb: the Word "became" flesh. There is no sense here of mere appearance or feint, as if the eternal *logos* looked as though it were flesh for a while and people could have been excused for thinking that it really was flesh. It was the *logos* in person that "dwelt among us" (v. 14)—not his proxy, his shadow, or a symbol of his presence.

This teaching that the Word became flesh and dwelt among us gives the biblical thinker an epistemology that diagonalizes the positions that Derrida rejects and proposes. To understand this, we need to consider briefly the way in which the incarnation contributes to a redefinition of transcendence and immanence in a biblical frame. First of all, the notion of transcendence that has been handed down through Neoplatonism equates God's transcendence with inaccessibility and unknowability, as John Frame explains:

> Historically, terrible problems have developed with concepts of transcendence and immanence. The transcendence of God (His exaltation, His mysteriousness) has been understood as God's being infinitely removed from the creation, being so far from us, so different from us, so "wholly other" and "wholly hidden" that we can have no knowledge of Him and

can make no true statements about Him. Such a god, therefore, has not revealed—and perhaps cannot reveal—himself
to us. (*DKG*, 13)

This notion of transcendence is going too far for Derrida, of
course, for to affirm that God is infinitely removed from the
world, or indeed to affirm that anything is infinitely removed
from us, is to say too much, for we must already know *that* it is
infinitely removed. If I know that something is unknowable, I
must know the unknowable *as* unknowable, which is to know
something about it. That is why Derrida hedges his talk of justice and so forth with the insistence on the little phrase "if there
is such a thing" ("s'il y en a"), a much more circumspect and
hesitant statement than "There most certainly is such a thing,
and what's more I can confidently affirm that I cannot know it."
Nevertheless, with this caveat, it is still correct to say that, for
Derrida, the "wholly other" is unknowable and that all statements we make about it are violent and liable to revision; it
cannot be assimilated to the economy of code, calculation, and
law. Frame continues:

> Similarly, the concept of immanence has been distorted in
> non-Christian thought, even in some would-be Christian the-
> ologies. Immanence has been understood to mean that God
> is virtually indistinguishable from the world, that when God
> enters the world He becomes so "worldly" that He cannot be
> found. The "Christian atheists" used to say that God aban-
> doned His divinity and no longer exists as God. Less "rad-
> ical" thinkers, like Barth and Bultmann, argued that though
> God still exists, His activity cannot be identified in space and
> time, that it affects all times and places equally and none in
> particular. Thus, in effect, there is no revelation; we have no
> responsibility before God. (*DKG*, 13–14)

Once more, this needs tweaking in Derrida's case because for Derrida everything exists under the condition of différance, and therefore there can be no pure immanence. The wholly other is never immanent in the sense of being fully present to consciousness in a codifiable, determinate way. If, as is impossible, it were, then it would lose its singularity and otherness and be reduced to a string of signifiers. However, what Derrida certainly cannot say is anything to the effect that justice or the pure gift "dwelt among us."

These notions of transcendence and immanence, even in their modified Derridean forms, are not what the Bible means when it talks either about God being exalted above us (transcendence) or being close to us (immanence). Frame explains that the idea of God's transcendence in the Bible cannot be taken to mean that he is far removed from us, because that would suggest he can be contained in some "other place" called heaven, whereas Solomon says that "heaven and the highest heaven cannot contain you" (1 Kings 8:27) (*DG*, 105). When the Bible talks about God being "exalted" and "lifted up," Frame argues, it is evoking his "royal dignity": "He is 'exalted,' not mainly as someone living far beyond the earth, but as one who sits on a throne. The expressions of transcendence refer to God's rule, his kingship, his lordship" (*DG*, 105). This idea of transcendence as covenant headship emphasizes God's control and authority, not his alienation from us, and is therefore "as far removed as possible from any notion of God as 'wholly other' or as 'infinitely distant'" (*DKG*, 16). As for immanence, when the Bible talks about God being "close by" or "present" with his people, the emphasis is on his "covenant solidarity" with his people, a relationship expressed most profoundly in the recurring biblical refrain "I will be your God and you shall be my people."

One implication of this biblical understanding of transcendence and immanence is that there is no tension or opposition between the transcendent God and the immanent God. His transcendence does not compromise his immanence, and his immanence does not void his transcendence:

> If God is covenant *head*, then He is exalted above His people; He is transcendent. If He is *covenant* head, then He is deeply involved with them; He is immanent. Note how beautifully these two concepts fit together when understood biblically. (*DKG*, 13)

So once again we find that two ideas which, for Derrida, cannot in the final analysis be combined, namely, (1) the absolute otherness that lays ethical demands upon me, and (2) codified, propositional rules, are, when biblically understood, of equal ultimacy and in harmony with each other.

Taking into account these differences between Derridean and biblical notions of transcendence and immanence, however, Derrida would still be uncomfortable with the biblical concept of incarnation, and specifically with the idea that the incarnation was a particular event at a particular moment in history, revealing God to a particular community (and, by implication, not to others),[8] or, in more Derridean language, the idea that the absolute could be fully present in its "trace" (a condition of being neither fully present nor utterly absent). This is part of a broader Derridean aversion to particularity in favor of the universal and the abstract, which we will discuss below in relation to Derrida's messianicity without messianism.

From a position associated with Radical Orthodoxy, Catherine Pickstock criticizes Derrida for "insistence on the transcendental writtenness of language," which "is revealed to

---

8. Steven Shakespeare makes this point in *Derrida and Theology* (London: T & T Clark, 2009), 168.

be, after all, a rationalistic gesture which suppresses embodiment and temporality."[9] This is not quite right. It is not the "written-ness of language" that is the problem for Derrida, for, as we have seen, the "text" is much broader than writing and arche-writing is not writtenness. What is deficient in Derrida's vision, and the reason why the incarnation of the absolute is impossible in his thought, is that his impersonalistic starting point prevents him from thinking the possibility that the material could be absolute. The absolute must always be abstract, in a way that has more in common with Platonic thought than the Bible. Building on this critique of Derrida (and building on this realignment of Pickstock's reading of Derrida), it is important to point out that, once again, the Bible diagonalizes the particular and the univer-sal in the same way that it does the one and the many.

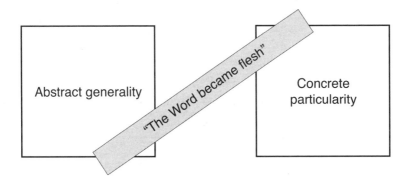

Fig. 5.5. The Incarnation Diagonalizes Abstract Generality and Concrete Particularity

We have already seen this in the case of absolute personality theism. God is personal (or rather, three particular persons) and also universal (he is God everywhere and of everyone) and

9. Catherine Pickstock, *After Writing: On the Liturgical Consummation of Philosophy* (Oxford: Blackwell, 1997), 4.

absolute (he cannot be reduced to anything more simple than himself, or prior to himself). In order to be absolute and universal, he does not need to be abstract, and in order to be personal he does not need to lose his absoluteness or universality. In the same way, in relation to the incarnation, Christ's particularity does not void his universality and make him into a local deity, as the promises given to Abraham in Genesis 12 make clear. There is no trade-off between universality and particularity in the biblical account, just as there is no trade-off between unity and plurality.

Christ came to the Jews as a Jew, but that does not mean that he is "owned" by a particular tradition, as if the particular has triumphed over the universal. A powerful pattern of the failure of any such attempt to co-opt God into a particular tradition is given in Joshua 5, where Joshua, the commander of the Israelite army, encounters "the commander of the army of the LORD":

> When Joshua was by Jericho, he lifted up his eyes and looked, and behold, a man was standing before him with his drawn sword in his hand. And Joshua went to him and said to him, "Are you for us, or for our adversaries?" And he said, "No, but I am the commander of the army of the LORD. Now I have come." And Joshua fell on his face to the earth and worshiped and said to him, "What does my lord say to his servant?" (Josh. 5:13–14)

Joshua's tentative attempt to situate God in terms of human categories and allegiances (for us or against us?) is overturned, in the space of one verse, into God situating Joshua as his worshipful servant.

There remains a further problem to be addressed in relation to the incarnation, one of which Derrida is keenly aware: how can the absolute (God) communicate with the finite (creature)?

How can human language or human experience do justice to that which is infinitely beyond language and experience, to the "wholly other"? To schematize this problem and begin to suggest a biblical response, we might express it as "How can flesh capture the Word?" In other words, how can finite human reality do justice to the absolute and infinite? Here, I think, the Bible is in agreement with Derrida: flesh cannot capture the Word. Even our most inspired human imaginings or formulations are laughably inadequate to do justice to God, who insists,

> My thoughts are not your thoughts,
> > neither are your ways my ways, declares the LORD.
> For as the heavens are higher than the earth,
> > so are my ways higher than your ways
> > and my thoughts than your thoughts. (Isa. 55:8–9)

However, the biblical claim is of course not that the flesh has captured the Word, that human language or experience has managed, after all, to capture something of God, but rather that the Word has become flesh and God has taken it upon himself to reveal himself in human language "top-down," as we might say, rather than "bottom-up." Interestingly, the passage from Isaiah just quoted continues in the following way:

> For as the rain and the snow come down from heaven
> > and do not return there but water the earth,
> making it bring forth and spout,
> > giving seed to the sower and bread to the eater,
> so shall my word be that goes out from my mouth;
> > it shall not return to me empty,
> but it shall accomplish that which I purpose,
> > and shall succeed in the thing for which I sent it. (Isa. 55:10–11)

God's thoughts and his ways are infinitely above ours, to be sure, but the same God has spoken words that are adequate to accomplish all his purposes in the world, including his purpose of revealing himself. The same idea of a top-down solution supervening on a bottom-up impossibility is found in Paul's letter to the Corinthians:

"What no eye has seen, nor ear heard,
     nor the heart of man imagined,
what God has prepared for those who love him"—
these things God has revealed to us through the Spirit.
     (1 Cor. 2:9–10)

As one final example, perhaps the most compact articulation of this idea is in Colossians 1, where Paul affirms that Christ is "the image of the invisible God" (Col. 1:15). It is a short phrase that rewards much reflection. Within the Reformed tradition, this top-down solution to the problem of the adequacy of human language to communicate the absolute God has been given the name "accommodation." The term was coined by Calvin in his *Institutes of the Christian Religion* (though he uses it only as a verb and not a noun), first to refute those who think that, when the Bible talks about God striking his enemies with his right hand, we must take that to mean that he has a physical body:

The Anthropomorphites also, who dreamed of a corporeal God, because mouth, ears, eyes, hands, and feet, are often ascribed to him in Scripture, are easily refuted. For who is so devoid of intellect as not to understand that God, in so speaking, lisps with us as nurses are wont to do with little children?

Such modes of expression, therefore, do not so much

express what kind of a being God is, as accommodate the knowledge of him to our feebleness. In doing so, he must, of course, stoop far below his proper height.[10]

It is important to understand what is being claimed in this doctrine of accommodation and what is not. Calvin is clear that: (1) It is God who does the accommodating, not us (*Institutes*, 1.13.1). (2) Accommodation is necessitated by our incapacity to comprehend, not by God's incapacity to express (1.17.13). (3) There is an important sense in which accommodated language represents God "not as he really is, but as we conceive of him" (1.17.13). In other words, God does not reveal himself to us in such a way that we can know him in the same way that he knows himself. (4) Accommodation facilitates our understanding of ourselves and of God, rather than frustrating it (2.16.2). (5) To speak in an accommodated way is not to speak falsely (2.16.2), and when we know God as he has accommodated himself to our understanding, we know the real God and not some model or shadow.

One crucial implication of this view is that the problem of making accommodation work, if we may put it this way, is God's and not ours. According to the doctrine of accommodation, it is God's problem to express himself in such an accommodated way that his word achieves his purposes in the world, and whereas such a task would be far beyond human ingenuity, it is not beyond the infinite God, as B. B. Warfield insists in *The Inspiration and Authority of the Bible*:

There is no ground for imagining that God is unable to frame His own message in the language of the organs of His revelation without its thereby ceasing to be, because expressed

10. Calvin, *Institutes*, 1.13.1 (translated by Henry Beveridge, 1845).

in a fashion natural to these organs, therefore purely His message.[11]

The burden of proof is on the one who presumes to know that this is impossible for God. To assume that human beings can speak adequately of God would be arrogance and hubris; to assume that God cannot speak adequately of himself would be presumption and just as arrogant.

Derrida brings to his reflections on language and violence the assumption, widely shared by those who insist upon the impossibility of speaking meaningfully about the transcendent, that language originates wholly on the human side of the equation. This should not be an assumption shared by one seeking to think biblically. In *The Doctrine of God*, John Frame insists that our words (for example, "righteousness") do not begin life in a purely naturalistic context and then get stretched and contorted to apply to God. To suggest that this is the case is to have a predilection for naturalism and to assume that all knowledge and culture are fundamentally and originally naturalistic, a position belied by the study of world cultures and civilizations. Language is just as much a part of God's creation as those other immaterial elements included in the "all things" created by and for Christ, according to Colossians 1, and summed up as "visible and invisible, whether thrones or dominions or rulers or authorities" (Col. 1:16). This does not mean that language provides a perfect representation of God in this fallen world, any more than thrones, rulers, or authorities are perfect pictures today of God's sovereign rule. What it does mean is that language has been made by and for Christ, and so we have no warrant to talk about "human language" as if this were something utterly alien

---

11. Benjamin B. Warfield, *The Inspiration and Authority of the Bible* (Philadelphia: Presbyterian and Reformed, 1967), 93.

to God's purpose in accommodating himself. Furthermore, the human person itself is not alien to God but, quite the contrary, made "in the image of God" (Gen. 1:27). This means that "we may speak anthropomorphically of God, because he has theomorphized man" (*DG*, 367). Humanity is already in the image of God, so to speak about God using human images is not unreasonable and, under the hermeneutical guidance and control of the images employed in the Bible, speaks truly of him. It is not that humans came first and sought to describe God in terms of themselves. God came first and made humans in terms of himself.

One further and very important point to make here is that God sets the purposes that his accommodated language seeks to achieve. We have already seen in the passage from Isaiah that God says that his word "shall accomplish that which I purpose," which may be quite different from what people may or may not desire it to accomplish. We also see this emphasis in Paul's encouragement to the young Timothy that "all Scripture is breathed out by God and profitable for teaching, for reproof, for correction, and for training in righteousness, that the man of God may be complete, equipped for every good work" (2 Tim. 3:16–17). It is the apostle's teaching that, with God's help, Timothy will be able to understand God's revelation in the Bible adequately for God's purposes. This final point, of course, is crucial; the verse does not say "all Scripture is breathed out by God and renders immediate the unitary and self-identical presence of the absolute in its trace." In this respect, the claim being made by biblical accommodation is a smaller one than the claim to the presence of the absolute in the trace that Derrida rejects, and the Bible would be quite happy to reject it along with him. What Derrida does not foresee—and this is the point at which, once more, the Bible diagonalizes the options he gives us—is that the absolute (God) would accommodate himself for purposes other than expressing absolute knowledge. The only thing about accommodation that prevents it from being laughable and dangerous is that God does it. Derrida is right that any human attempts to capture God in language will be dangerous and violent, but that is not the biblical claim.

In view of divine accommodation, therefore, it seems too hasty to conclude—along with theologian Graham Ward, who interacts profoundly and at length with Derrida's thought and has written an important book about Derrida and the theologian Karl Barth—that "a certain agnosticism must be preserved within theology, for God cannot be pinned down and defined."[12] This sounds a lot like Derrida, but not a lot like the Bible. To say things about God, especially if those are things that he has previously said about himself, is neither to pin him down nor to define him in a restrictive way. Content is not the enemy of freedom when it is the content of absolutely personal character. God is not pinned down by whom he reveals himself to be; he is not defined (in a negative sense) by his character. When Ward says that Christ, "like différance, transcends difference and metaphysical polarities and makes the movement of signification possible,"[13] he is evacuating Christ's revelation of God of determinate content, stripping it back to an indeterminate otherness that is necessary within a Derridean frame, in order to avoid totalizing violence, but this view is inimical to a biblical frame of reference.

Brute Facts, the Transcendental Signified, and Idolatry

Something further needs to be said about the way in which Christ reveals God in John 1. In verse 18, John writes: "No one has ever seen God; the only God, who is at the Father's side, he

---

12. Graham Ward, *Barth, Derrida and the Language of Theology* (Cambridge: Cambridge University Press, 1995), 244.
13. Ibid., 248.

has made him known." The verb for "made him known" here is *exegesato*, from which we get the English word *exegesis*. Other English translations of the New Testament have "explained," "related," or "declared." Christ has exegeted God, interpreted him, declared him. In other words, God is not presented to us as a bare, uninterpreted "fact." Our knowledge of God is not, in this sense, absolute or objective, and at this point the Bible and Derrida are agreed in condemning any pretensions to absolute (that is, uninterpreted) knowledge. Just as accommodation can reveal God "not as he really is" (to use Calvin's words), but still be true, so also can Christ reveal the real, unapproachable God, but not in a full-blown, face-to-face theophany. In Christ we see God, accommodated.

Derrida's rejection of claims to absolute knowledge was rehearsed at some length in the metaphysics section of the first half of this book. From a Reformed point of view, the desire for absolute, uninterpreted, and context-free knowledge—of God or anything else—is idolatrous and should not be the Christian's aim:

> We have no access to reality apart from our interpretative faculties. To seek such access is to seek release from crea-turehood. . . . We cannot step outside of our own skins. The desire for a "fact" totally devoid of human interpretation that can serve as an authoritative criterion for all interpretations is a non-Christian desire, a desire to substitute some other authority for the Word of God. (*DKG*, 71–72)

This condemnation of the idolatry of seeking absolute or objective (i.e., uninterpreted) knowledge is the area of reso-nance between Derrida's thought and the Bible that has been most usefully and profitably exploited by his Christian read-ers. In *Graven Ideologies*, Bruce Benson argues that "while it is true that the postmoderns themselves succumb to idolatry (as shall become clear), they are often particularly adept at identifying—and scathingly criticizing—idols created by both philosophers and theologians."[14] Despite this insight, Benson does sell the Bible short, I think, when he argues that, for Derrida, "justice cannot be justified by anything further"[15] and neither can a Christian view of justice based on God's character. First of all, Benson seems to be comparing apples with oranges, because Derrida's justice is in the final analysis indeterminate and God's character is content-rich, so to justify Derrida's justice is not to justify any particular action over any other. Secondly, this equivalence forgets the Creator-creature distinction: the important difference between Derrida and the Bible here must surely count for something (if not for everything), namely, the difference between Derrida's idea of an impossible justice as a condition of possibility within his view of the world that allows only one mode of being, and a biblical ethics issuing from God's character set within a view of the world in which he is ultimate and we are part of his creation. Thinking about justice in terms of God's character does not merely "push the problem back a step,"[16] or at least it does so only if the Creator-creature distinction is discounted, because in God's character ontology and ethics (the "is" and the "ought") are equally ultimate and not separate in the first place, requiring us to build a bridge from one to the other.

There is an important difference, though, between a biblical understanding of idolatry and its Derridean-inflected version. According to the Derridean version, a way of conceiving God is idolatrous if it is not deconstructed—that is to say, if it unequivocally affirms any determinate content in relation to

14. Bruce Ellis Benson, *Graven Ideologies: Nietzsche, Derrida and Marion on Modern Idolatry* (Downers Grove, IL: InterVarsity Press, 2002), 48.
15. Ibid., 140.
16. Ibid.

God. According to the biblical version, by contrast, a way of conceiving God is idolatrous if it does not conform to what God has revealed about himself. Derrida begins with deconstruction and thinks of God accordingly; the Bible begins with God as he has revealed himself, and thinks of everything else accordingly.

We can push further than this and explore how the biblical notion of idolatry provides a critique of Derrida's resistance to idolatrous concepts. From a biblical point of view, when we refuse to worship the God who has revealed himself, iconoclasm itself becomes an idolatry: something that we put in the place of God. We see the Bible diagonalizing Derrida's own position and the position he condemns, and grouping them together once more as variations on a theme. From a biblical point of view, both (1) Derrida's rejection of the claim that the God who is absolutely other can be made present in the trace, as well as (2) his own insistence on deconstructing such claims, are equally idolatrous, and the only way to avoid such idolatry is to accept God's self-revelation in the Bible.

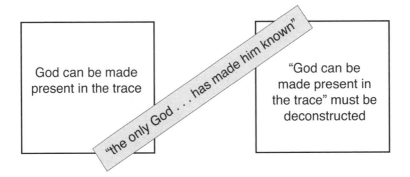

Fig. 5.6. The Incarnation Diagonalizes Idolatrous Claims about God's Presence

It is possible to be idolatrous by refusing God's self-revelation in a resolute affirmation that we cannot or should not claim to know what God is like, just as much as it is idolatrous to worship something else in place of God. There is an idolatry of ignorance as well as an idolatry of knowledge. Derrida is somewhat hoist by his own petard at this point. He knows for sure, before he has encountered the Christian revelation, that any determinate articulation of doctrine will necessarily be idolatrous. He has immunized himself from being surprised by the God who speaks. Benson is aware of this when he critiques Derrida's rejection of any determinate content to faith, noting that he would lead us to be "so afraid of violence that we would eschew not only locks but texts and institutions and beliefs and practices themselves."[17]

Thus far in this section, I have been arguing that Derridean and Van Tilian thought share an aversion to claiming to speak of God in an absolute, brute, or uninterpreted way. There is also a second important resonance between Derrida and Van Til on the subject of brute fact, this time as it pertains to creation. We have already seen that, in Colossians 1, Paul argues that all things were created by Christ and for Christ. This means that all things (including ourselves) are always already interpreted, or, to put it in more Derridean terms, there is "nothing outside" the context of God's pre-interpretation. The world is not first of all an inert, indifferent, or meaningless environment that God subsequently chooses to infuse with meaning; materiality and meaning are— just like unity and plurality, and just like universality and particularity—of "equal ultimacy" in the biblical account of "all things." Frame explains:

> All facts have been interpreted by God, and since all things
> are what they are by virtue of God's eternal plan, we must
> say that "the interpretation of the facts precedes the facts"
> (Van Til). The idea of "brute fact" is an invention intended

17. Ibid., 164.

to furnish us with a criterion of truth other than God's revelation. (*DKG*, 71)

The bedrock or ground zero of reality for the Christian is not a world of brute, uninterpreted facts, but God's own interpretations, which are equally ultimate with the facts. Therefore, growth in knowledge is not an approximation to the objective and uninterpreted, but an ever-increasing approximation to God's own interpretations. This is the guarantee of intelligibility in the universe for the Christian, as Greg Bahnsen explains:

> The believer's attempt to organize and interpret his experience is successful when it reflects the original order of God's mind, by which all things are defined and all events work together; he seeks to "think God's thoughts after Him."[18]

Insofar as the claim for there to be something "outside the text" is the claim that such a thing stands as a brute, uninterpreted fact not dependent on or situated within any context that governs its meaning, Derrida's famous phrase is close to the Van Tilian rejection of the objectivist's idea of brute facts. While Derrida and Van Til are united here in opposing the objectivist appeal to brute facts, there is of course also a great difference between the two positions. For Van Til, a correct understanding of things is always to interpret them in line with God's own interpretation, whereas Derrida's "there is nothing outside the text" results in a radical openness to the meaning of things. Looked at from another angle, though, the difference is not as great as all that. Derrida and Van Til would be quite happy to agree, I think, that, in Van Til's terms, "The meaning of words derives from the

---

18. Greg L. Bahnsen, *Van Til's Apologetic: Readings and Analysis* (Philipsburg, NJ: P&R Publishing, 1998), 140n136.

total system of which they form a part" (*ICG*, 9). They would also agree that we cannot know that total system exhaustively. The difference (and it is a very great difference) is that for Van Til that system must include God's creation and authoritative pre-interpretation of the things of the universe, whereas for Derrida such a thing is unthinkable.

One final word here: we must be careful not to confuse this idea of God's pre-interpretation of the "facts" of the universe with a rigid, inflexible, hermeneutical straitjacket. To say that a tree or a library, for example, is "for Christ" is anything but a ban on thinking creatively about trees and libraries. On the contrary, it is an invitation to find a thousand and one ways in which our care and appreciation of trees and our use and fostering of libraries might be "for Christ." The Bible gives us the ultimate purpose and destination of "all things," but it is left to us to figure out creatively what that means for our thinking and action today.

Gift, Recognition, and Praise

Moving through John's prologue, we read in verse 16 that from Christ's fullness "we have all received, grace upon grace." How does the biblical idea of gift and grace relate to Derrida's account of the gift in *Given Time* and elsewhere? Derrida's account, it will be remembered, is analogous to his distinction between codified law and absolute justice in "Force of Law." Any gift that is calculated or reciprocated with a counter-gift enters an economy of exchange and barter and therefore loses its nature as a gift, and the only pure or absolute gift would be one that is not even recognized as a gift, for that is the only way that it can escape the tit-for-tat economy of gift exchange.

The first thing to notice here is that the gift of grace in John 1 and elsewhere is not like Derrida's absolute gift, because we know that "we have all received" it and we know at least to some extent what it is that we have received. Does this mean that the biblical idea of grace gets sucked into an economy of exchange between God and human beings, reducing salvation to a grubby business deal? The answer is no, but the reason is not because the gift remains absolute in Derrida's sense. Once more we find the Bible diagonalizing the two options that Derrida presents to us (absolute gift or economic reciprocation), cutting across them in a way for which Derrida's thought cannot account.

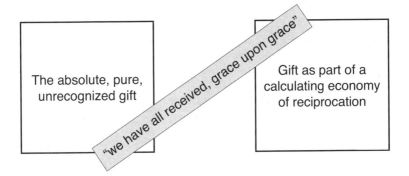

Fig. 5.7. God's Gift of Grace Diagonalizes Derrida's Account of the Gift

A particularly illuminating passage in trying to flesh out our biblical account of the gift is Paul's doxology in Romans 11:33–36:

> Oh, the depth of the riches and wisdom and knowledge of
>   God! How unsearchable are his judgments and how
>   inscrutable his ways!
> "For who has known the mind of the Lord,
>   or who has been his counsellor?"
> "Or who has given a gift to him
>   that he might be repaid?"
> For from him and through him and to him are all things.
>   To him be glory forever. Amen.

This passage is fascinating for the way in which it both resonates with and dissents from the positions laid out by Derrida. It resonates with Derrida's insistence upon otherness in its affirmation that God's judgments are unsearchable and his ways inscrutable. Paul concurs that we have not "pinned God down," to use a favorite image of some Christian readers of Derrida: we cannot predict what he will do in all situations. He surprises us. Furthermore, Paul in this passage affirms a sort of unilateralism that resonates with Derrida's absolute gift: none of us has given anything to God that would drag his gift of grace into an economy of exchange. Why not? Is not our very recognition of the gift of God's grace a minimal repayment and the inauguration of an economy of exchange, as Derrida argues in *Given Time*? No, because God owns everything to begin with, including the breath with which we thank him and the lips that sing his praise. He gives us the faith with which we believed in him, and he is sovereign over the thought that arose in our minds to thank him in the first place. This is the first thing to notice: recognizing God's gift as a gift and thanking him for it do not annul its status as a gift, because those who thus recognize and thank God are, at the same time, utterly dependent upon him for that very recognition and thanks. Nothing is given to God that was not already his and that he did not bring about. But we can go further, for the very doxology in which Paul is pointing out the impossibility of giving to God is also framed as a passage of praise to God. It is not only that God's gift remains a gift despite our giving thanks for it, but that the glory of that gift is enhanced and emphasized in the praise. This is the point made by Jonathan Edwards:

> So, God glorifies himself towards the creatures also [in] two ways: (1) by appearing to them, being manifested to their understanding; (2) in communicating himself

to their hearts, and in their rejoicing and delighting in, and enjoying the manifestations which he makes of himself. . . . God is glorified not only by his glory's being seen, but by its being rejoiced in. . . . When those that see it delight in it: God is more glorified than if they only see it; his glory is then received by the whole soul, both by the understanding and by the heart.[19]

For Derrida, to recognize a gift as a gift annuls the gift. In the case of biblical grace, however, for the recipient to recognize the gift and praise the giver only brings glory to the latter and a joy to the former, without reducing the gift to a logic of reciprocity or exchange. This way in which grace ruptures the quid pro quo of reciprocal exchange can helpfully be called an "aneconomy," which is a way of thinking about giving that escapes the economic paradigm according to which a balance sheet is kept between giver and receiver, and which moves away from reciprocity in favor of mutuality.

Predestination and Messianicity without Messianism

The great concern of Derrida's messianicity without messianism is to keep the present open to a future, the arrival of which will be "monstrous"—in other words, not within our current horizon of expectation. On the surface, it would seem that biblical Christianity is at loggerheads with this openness. The idea in John 1 that those who belong to Christ are not born "of the will of man," but of God, is amplified elsewhere.

---

19. Jonathan Edwards, *The "Miscellanies,"* edited by Thomas Schafer, in *The Works of Jonathan Edwards*, vol. 13 (New Haven: Yale University Press, 1994), 495.

In Ephesians 1, for example, Christians are said to be "predestined . . . for adoption as sons through Jesus Christ, according to the purpose of his will" (Eph. 1:5). Nothing could seem further from a radically open and monstrous future than a God who predestines "before the foundation of the world" (Eph. 1:4) those who will be saved.

The question we need to ask is whether this predestination has the consequences that Derrida fears, namely, that the future will be merely a linear progression from the assumptions of the present and that we lose our ability to be surprised or confronted by radical otherness. At the risk of trying the reader's patience, I suggest one last time that the biblical position diagonalizes Derrida's thought at this point. Derrida presents us with two options: radical openness to the monstrous future or preprogrammed predictability. From a biblical point of view, however, Derrida's own openness is just as closed as the predictability he condemns, and the only truly open option is biblical predestination.

First of all, in what sense is Derrida's openness closed? To help us respond to this question, I want to draw on the work of Catherine Malabou, who collaborated closely with Derrida on the book *Counterpath* and whose own philosophy of "plasticity" is elaborated as a sometimes-dissonant counterpoint to Derrida's deconstruction. In distinguishing Derridean deconstruction from her own plasticity, Malabou describes deconstruction as a tic, a gesture that is performed with a certain preprogrammed predictability.[20] Derrida, of course, would strongly object to this characterization, and I pointed out above that the constant refreshing of his vocabulary is an attempt to avoid just this sort of criticism. However, a deconstructive

20. See Catherine Malabou, *La chambre du milieu: De Hegel aux neurosciences* (Paris: Éditions Hermann, 2009), 287.

reading of a text still remains predictable in its broad outline, and there is, despite Derrida's efforts, something of a method about deconstruction. Malabou's plasticity incorporates moments of both transformation and stasis, proliferation and destruction, whereas Derrida will always deconstruct the metaphysics of presence. He says as much in *The Problem of Genesis in Husserl's Philosophy*:

> It is always a question of an originary complication of the origin, of an initial contamination of the simple, of an inaugural divergence that no analysis could present, make present in its phenomenon or reduce to the pointlike nature of the element, instantaneous and identical to itself. (*PG*, xv)

In the same way, Derrida's messianicity without messianism will always insist upon the structural rather than the determinate, upon openness rather than closure. If openness is the ability to be surprised, then Derrida's "openness" is not itself open: it knows that the to-come will be monstrous and that it cannot be anything else. It knows, for example, that God cannot reveal himself in determinate terms.

There is also a sense in which Derrida's insistence upon openness to the to-come neutralizes all singular otherness and reduces it to the same indeterminacy. Catherine Pickstock is uneasy with Derridean otherness, which she characterizes as "an autonomous word which conceals or violently eradicates its origins and dictates to its 'author,' rendering him entirely passive before a disembodied and (spiritual?) power."[21] We encountered above Martin Hägglund's argument that Derrida's openness is so indeterminate that he cannot foreclose the possibility that what will come will in fact be evil, because "the

---

21. Pickstock, *After Writing*, 22.

other can be anything whatsoever or anyone whosoever and one cannot know in advance how one should act in relation to him, her, or it."[22] By insisting only upon openness and unknowability, Derrida is, in an indirect way, dictating what God must be like, because unknowability and indeterminacy are not positive attributes of God, but the absence of determinate positive attributes.

If Derridean openness is closed in these ways, can biblical predestination fare any better? The answer will take a little while to unpack, and I beg the reader's indulgence. First, we can note that the radical indeterminacy (Pickstock's critique) and therefore the indifference to horror or evil (Hägglund's critique) of Derrida's messianicity without messianism is not shared by biblical eschatology, for in the biblical account the contours of God's character frame and shape what is to come. There is a certain determinate content to the Christian account of otherness from the beginning, or even before the beginning, because the relations between the three persons of the Trinity are presented in the Bible, not as abstract, empty, or formal relations, but as content-rich relations of love (John 3:35; 17:24). Father, Son, and Spirit are not just related to each other in an indeterminate way; their relations have a specific content, namely, that they love each other, and this decisively affects the Christian idea of otherness, not as generic or undetermined difference, but as, most fundamentally, loving solicitude. What is to come is shaped by God's character, not only by his abstract otherness. We know, for example, that heaven (or to use more biblical language, the New Jerusalem) will be a place where we will see God face-to-face and where there will be no more mourning, crying, or pain, rather than a place of estrangement from God

---

22. Martin Hägglund, *Radical Atheism: Derrida and the Time of Life* (Stanford: Stanford University Press, 2008), 31.

and of weeping and gnashing of teeth. Nevertheless, and equally importantly, it is as vain for us to seek to discern exactly how the character traits that God has revealed will be embodied and will shape that existence as it would be for a two-dimensional being to imagine existence in three dimensions. There is a sense, then, in which the biblical to-come is quite predictable, and another sense in which it is utterly unpredictable and sure to confound any feeble human attempts to comprehend it ahead of time, which is perhaps one reason why the book of Revelation evokes rather than describes it. As in the case of the Trinity, what emerges from the biblical account is not the privileging of unknowing over knowing—as in Derrida we saw the privileging of arche-difference over identity—nor the reverse, which would characterize a rationalist or "modernist" account of God. Rather, there is an equal ultimacy of the predictable and the unpredictable: "What no eye has seen, nor ear heard . . . God has revealed" (1 Cor. 2:9). We know just what heaven will be like (we will see God face-to-face) and, at the same time, we have no idea what heaven will be like.

Is Christian eschatology "planned out" or "scripted" in advance, like the calculable future that for Derrida is unable to provide a meaningful change from the present? Yes and no. From God's perspective, yes, because Christ, the crucified Lamb, was "foreknown before the foundation of the world" (1 Peter 1:20). But from a human point of view, the cross was hardly calculable or in linear continuity with people's expectations of a messiah. It was so outside the general horizon of expectation, in fact, that only a small number of people believed in the crucified Savior; many ridiculed the very idea, and the authorities at the time put him to death. In this way, the cross was "monstrous" in Derrida's sense, and for unbelievers today it still remains outside the horizon of expectation, outside "the sort of thing that any God I could believe in would do."

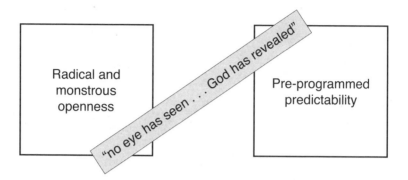

Fig. 5.8. The Bible Diagonalizes Derrida's Opposition between Radical Openness and Scripted Closure

Does predestination rob humanity of creativity, as the Derridean dichotomy of preprogrammed predictability and openness would suggest? Van Til argues that, far from trapping humanity in the predictable outworking of a scripted plot, predestination is the precondition of human creativity. The alternative to the sovereignty of God is the sovereignty of chance (both "inside," in the human reasoning and brain, and "outside" in the world), and chance thwarts all human creative aspirations:

> As Christians we hold that determinate human experience could work to no end, could work in accordance with no plan, and could not even get under way, if it were not for the existence of the absolute will of God. It is on this ground then that we hold to the absolute will of God as the presupposition of the will of man. Looked at in this way, that which to many seems at first glance to be the greatest hindrance to moral responsibility, namely the conception of an absolutely sovereign God, becomes the very foundation of its possibility. (*CTE*, 83)

It is too hasty simply to say that predestination is closure, the opposite of Derrida's openness, because the Bible affirms both predestination and human responsibility. The Creator-creature distinction is of central importance here, for it marks the difference between Derrida insisting that one logic must obtain for all of reality and the Bible's willingness to acknowledge that truths which appear to us to be contrary are both affirmed in relation to God. Predestination is incompatible with human creativity only if we start with the assumption that God's thoughts are our thoughts and his ways our ways—in other words, that he is transparent to our understanding. The Bible does not start with that assumption, and is therefore happy for predestination and human creativity to sit side by side.

There is one further point to make about Derrida's messianicity without messianism, for in rejecting all determinate messianisms and seeking to discern an underlying structure of messianicity that they all share, Derrida is manifesting a preference for the structural and formal over the determinate, which, though we have mentioned it before now, we have not assessed directly. This preference for the structural over the determinate, for messianicity over particular messianisms, is in opposition to absolute personality theism, for which the things that are true of God are not true of him as one instance of a greater truth or phenomenon. When we talk about God's goodness, for example, it is not that God is one expression of the abstract concept of goodness that exists apart from him and is broader and more original than he is. Rather, ultimate reality is personal, and abstract concepts are derived from God's original and absolute personality.

God does not supervene upon or intervene within a field of possibilities that precedes him. He himself comes before everything, including fields, possibilities, structures, and virtualities. God is therefore not derived from, situated within, or reducible to anything more originary or fundamental than he is. The coming of Jesus Christ as Messiah is not one contingent instance of a more fundamental, structural messianism, from which it can be separated like a contingent husk from its structural kernel. Christ as Messiah comes first, and any structural messianicity that may be inferred from his coming is always subsequent to, and indeed directly contingent upon, him who "upholds the universe by the word of his power" (Heb. 1:3). Christ the Messiah is the origin of, and is more fundamental and originary than, the structure of messianicity.

From the point of view of comparative cultural criticism, however, we can go further still and say more than this, for the preference for the general over the particular, for the structural over the determinate is, in fact, a particular and historically situated preference, informed by the inclination toward abstract universality and formalism that owes much to the eighteenth-century Enlightenment and its cultural legacy. To see the structural as more fundamental than the particular is a judgment that betrays its own cultural particularity, its own genealogy. It is, as we have already seen, a judgment that the Bible, with its insistence on the equal ultimacy of particularity and universality, does not share.

Union with Christ and "I Am Just"

As we draw to the end of our consideration of Derrida's ethical thought in the light of John's prologue and in the light of Van Tilian Reformed philosophy, we turn now to the question of (self-)righteousness. In "Force of Law," Derrida is at pains to foreclose any possibility of being able to say "I know that I am just" (FL, 245), because such a claim to absolute justice here and now would give warrant to even the grossest atrocities on the part of the one who considers himself absolutely just. In order to guard against this possibility, Derrida insists that we can never know that we are just. In John's prologue, by contrast, the evangelist has no qualms in including his Christian readers alongside himself in the "we" who have received God's grace and therefore become, in the words of verse 12, "children of God." In the context of our current discussion, this claim is put more pointedly still in Colossians 1, where Paul writes to his readers that "you, who once were alienated and hostile in mind, doing evil deeds, he has now reconciled in his body of flesh by his death, in order to present you holy and blameless and above reproach before him" (Col. 1:21–22). Whether this blamelessness is current at the time of writing or eschatological for Paul does not concern us here. In either case, the Bible seems much more ready to talk about justice and righteousness for specific people than Derrida is comfortable with. The question follows: does this talk of being "blameless and above reproach" before God (no less!) open the door to the sort of abuses that Derrida fears will flow from the proclamation that "I am just"?

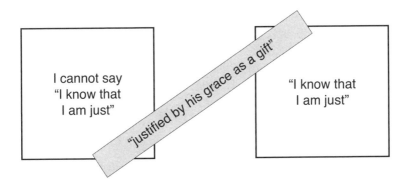

Fig. 5.9. Grace Diagonalizes Derrida's Opposition between Claiming "I Am Just" and Refusing to Make Any Such Claim

The Bible once more diagonalizes Derrida's two options, neither refusing all talk of justice in the present nor asserting "I am just" in the way in which Derrida uses the phrase. For Derrida, the two options are either to be just on one's own account or to recognize that one cannot know that one is just on one's own account. The Bible introduces a third possibility: I know that I am just, but that justice does not have its source in me and does not permit me to arrogate to myself any authority that would lead to violent acts, but in fact cements and underlines my own inability to act on my own account. The dynamics of this diagonalization are perhaps most clearly set out in Romans 3:22–28:

> There is no distinction: for all have sinned and fall short of the glory of God, and are justified by his grace as a gift, through the redemption that is in Christ Jesus, whom God put forward as a propitiation by his blood, to be received by faith. This was to show God's righteousness, because in his divine forbearance he had passed over former sins. It was to show his righteousness at the present time, so that he might be just and the justifier of the one who has faith in Jesus. Then what becomes of our boasting? It is excluded. By what kind of law? By a law of works? No, but by the law of faith. For we hold that one is justified by faith apart from works of the law.

To be able to claim that "I am just" in Derrida's sense would, in Paul's language, be to be righteous by a "law of works": to be able to claim on one's own account, and by one's own judgment of oneself, that one is righteous. So far, Paul and Derrida are in agreement. But Paul introduces another dynamic into the question of righteousness, namely, justification that is received "by his grace as a gift," not self-proclaimed—a righteousness that involves two people, a giver and a receiver, and not just an "I." To try to splice the Derridean and Pauline vocabularies together, Romans 3 is claiming that Christ, the only one who can justly claim that "I am just," propitiates God's anger against all the unrighteous who receive his gift of righteousness by faith, such that for those who are united to Christ, it is now just that they be treated as just, under Christ's headship. What the Christian can say, therefore, on the authority of God's Word, is that "Christ is just, and I am just in him." Alive to the very kind of danger that Derrida wants to foreclose by barring the pronouncement that "I am just," Paul immediately goes on to insist that such a vicarious righteousness undercuts all possibility of boasting (and, *a fortiori*, all possibility of acting as one who can do no wrong). The notion of vicarious righteousness undercuts Derrida's alternatives and provides a righteousness that does not bring with it an authorization to bring justice at the tip of the sword or through the barrel of a gun, and does not write the one who is just a blank check to do whatever they want. Derrida presents us with a dichotomy between the absolute tyranny of "I am just" and an indefinite postponement of justice. Biblical Christianity cuts across this dichotomy and opens another possibility, which both affirms justice and, in the same move, undercuts tyranny or self-righteousness. The church, to its shame, has frequently appropriated this biblical teaching as a roundabout way of saying "I am just" in Derrida's sense, claiming in this or that war that God is "on our side," for example, but to understand Romans 3 is to understand that this is an abuse of the passage. God, as we have seen, is "neither" for Joshua's army nor against it (Josh. 5:13–14); his legions of angels follow no human orders.

CONCLUSION

I hope that I have done enough in these pages to make at least a plausible case that the future of Reformed scholarship in dialogue with Derrida can be fruitfully pursued in the Van Tilian tradition. I have only been able here to scratch the surface of the similarities and differences between Derrida and Van Til, and it is my hope that others will explore further the myriad resonances and dissonances in their two bodies of work. It is also my hope that the way I have grouped my observations and interactions with Derrida's thought around the two motifs of "equal ultimacy" and "diagonalization" will provide tools for Christian scholars to continue engaging with Derrida and other thinkers besides him—tools that will themselves, I hope, be critiqued and refined.

To sum up the relation between Derrida's thought and biblical Christianity as articulated in the Van Tilian tradition, I would say that the biblical view of God repeatedly takes the categories of deconstruction by surprise, offering the reality of God neither as the self-identical presence that deconstruction seeks to show to be illusory, nor as its own différance or arche-writing. Biblical Christianity does not confine itself within the concepts, movements, and possibilities that deconstruction maps out. On the contrary, it shows that both the positions that Derrida rejects and his own views share much in common, and it contests those common assumptions. If one begins with the assumptions of deconstruction, one cannot end with biblical Christianity, and if one begins with the assumptions of biblical Christianity, one does not end with deconstruction. In this sense, there is an antithesis between the two that more Christian readers of Derrida would do well to recognize. This by no means leads to the conclusion that Christians have nothing to learn from deconstruction, as I hope also to have shown, and other Christian readers of Derrida would do well to acknowledge this.

A position that holds to the equal ultimacy of the one and the many; that sees ultimate reality as personal, Trinitarian, and loving; and that has at its heart a logic of grace that undermines all pretensions to self-righteous violence, is simply not on the radar of deconstruction. In offering his own "yes, but" to deconstruction, the cross-bearing Christ who justifies the ungodly is the messianic "scandal," the coming of whom is so otherwise to all reasonable or possible expectations that it is too much for even the writer of *The Gift of Death* to accept. For one final time, we must affirm that biblical Christianity does not fulfill Derrida's messianicity of the coming of the monstrous, but it does not straightforwardly confound it either. Biblical Christianity opposes deconstructive messianicity, as deconstruction itself opposes the logic of presence and identity, neither straightforwardly affirming it nor simply rejecting it. Deconstruction does not see biblical Christianity coming.

GLOSSARY

absolute personality theism. A theme of Hermann Bavinck's thought (in volume 2 of his *Reformed Dogmatics*), taken up by Van Til and further developed by Frame, according to which the biblical revelation of God is marked out from all other religions by claiming that God is both absolute and personal, and that these two fundamental truths about him are not in conflict with one another. See also *equal ultimacy*.

aneconomy. A term to designate the breaking or subverting of rules of reciprocal exchange. Grace is aneconomic because it does not operate according to the rules of the market in which goods exchanged are of equal value.

aporia. Etymologically, *aporia* means "something that does not allow passage" (FL, 244). In "Force of Law," Derrida argues that a true decision (as opposed to following rules mechanically) requires the experience of aporia, the experience of the impossibility of making a just decision on the basis of calculation alone.

arche-writing. An originary non-self-presence that provides the shared condition of possibility of writing and speech.

Like writing, arche-writing lacks the supposed immediacy of meaning in speech, and so Derrida is arguing that immediacy and presence are constructs and not original. Near-synonym for *différance*.

as-structure of being. In Heidegger's thought, the world is not present to our consciousness as an immediate presence of matter (solids, liquids, gasses), but as objects and entities that already have meanings in the human world. For example, I experience a chair, not as an agglomeration of brute matter, but as a thing for sitting on and a sign of civilization. The as-structure of being refers to the fact that, under normal circumstances, I cannot come out from under these cultural meanings and symbols in my experience of the world: I experience everything as what it is for me.

binary opposition. An opposition between two elements, one of which, for Derrida, is privileged over the other in an unwarranted way. Examples: presence/absence, male/female, speech/writing, inside/outside. Derrida shows that binary oppositions deconstruct themselves because the privileged term relies on the subordinate term for its own definition.

condition of possibility. A term coined by Kant in the context of his transcendental thought. Rather than asking, "What exists?" Kant asks, "What is it necessary to suppose or assume in order to account for the experiences we have?" Both Derrida and Van Til make use of transcendental thinking.

deconstruction. One of a number of terms used by Derrida to describe "what happens" (TOJ, 17) in written texts and in meanings and experience more broadly. It has come to be used as a general description of Derrida's thought, though he resisted this and preferred to use a new vocabulary for each of his singular encounters with texts. The word *deconstructionism* is not used by Derrida and implies that deconstruction can be reduced to a static method.

différance. For Derrida, the mode of existence of everything that exists. In major strands of traditional Western metaphysics, things exist as isolated atoms, their meanings completely present to our consciousness. Derrida argues that this is a theological illusion and that, rather than being completely present, things exist as always different from themselves and deferred with respect to themselves (the two senses of the French *différer*). A near-synonym of *arche-writing*.

double bind. In Derrida's ethics, the twin absolute injunctions (1) to respond immediately and exhaustively to the demand that comes from the other, and (2) not to do violence to the other by assuming to know what their demand means. It is violent to respond (because no response is perfect and I never do full justice to the other), and it is violent to fold one's arms and do nothing.

equal ultimacy. In Van Til's thought, the biblical teaching that, in the Trinitarian God, neither unity nor plurality is prior to, or reducible to, the other.

Frame, John (born 1939). North American Reformed philosopher and theologian, sharing many of the characteristics of presuppositional apologetics with *Cornelius Van Til*. In his four-volume Theology of Lordship series and elsewhere Frame deals at length, among many other themes, with *absolute-personality theism*, the creator-creature distinction, and *transcendence/immanence*. See also *equal ultimacy*.

iterability. A term used by Derrida to describe the condition of language. Combining the senses of the Latin *iter* ("again") and Sanskrit *itara* ("other"), to say that language is iterable means that it repeats words (e.g., one word, such as *dog*, can designate any number of singular entities in the world) but never does so exactly, because the context of each use of a word differs (sometimes ever so slightly) from every other context.

justice. In Derrida's ethics and politics, justice is the absolute demand that a decision or judgment take exhaustive account of all aspects of the singularity of a case or situation, rather than just following rules. A judgment seeking to be just must calculate, but it must also pass through the aporia of decision. It is impossible to be sure that one has done this (perhaps some new evidence will come to light?), and so Derrida hedges his use of the term with the caveat "if there is such a thing" (FL, 243). It is impossible to say that "I know that I am just" (FL, 245). See also *law, aporia.*

law. In Derrida's ethics and politics, law (*droit*) is the calculable, codifiable statute that can be set down in black and white. Because simply following the law does not take account of the singularity of unique circumstances, it will never lead to justice being done. See also *justice.*

logocentrism. A term used by Derrida to describe the traditional Western understanding of truth, according to which an absolute and self-present *logos* grounds all truth and acts as a *transcendental signified.* For logocentrism, truth is to be found outside language, and language is a tool that can be thrown away once it has brought us to an immediate understanding of truth. The "epoch of the logos" (*OG,* 12) began with Plato's ideas—fixed, eternal Forms that guaranteed the meaning of the changing and particular entities in the world—and is only now coming to an end. See also *metaphysics of presence, phonocentrism.*

messianicity without messianism. One of a series of terms with the structure "x without x" in Derrida's later thought, which indicates the wish to keep the structure or force of a particular way of thinking while evacuating it of stable or determinate content. Derrida's messianicity without messianism keeps the structure of the to-come and the openness to the future of Jewish, Christian, and Marxist messianisms, while refusing to designate what or who it is that will come, other than saying it will confound our expectations.

metaphysics of presence. For Derrida, the traditional way of conducting metaphysics in the West, holding that things exist as fully present to our consciousness and that identity is prior to difference. Derrida shows how this way of thinking deconstructs itself. See also *logocentrism, phonocentrism, binary opposition*.

ontotheology. From the Greek *on* ("being"), *theos* ("God"), and *logos* ("study"), a term used by Martin Heidegger to discuss a philosophical tradition starting with Aristotle, which thinks of God as the totality of being, and/or as the salient example of being. The god of ontotheology is a "god of the philosophers," a concept and not a person.

phonocentrism. A term used by Derrida in *OG* to describe the Western philosophical privilege for the supposed immediacy of meaning in spoken language over the inferior mode of writing. Writing uses signs (written words), whereas speech is an unmediated expression of the speaker's thoughts. The Western understanding of truth in general, Derrida argues, rests on this presupposition of immediacy, but it is in fact an illusion. See also *metaphysics of presence*.

sign. In Saussure's linguistics, a term to describe the structure of meaning in language as the unity of a (sensible) signifier and its (intelligible) signified. See also *signifier, signified*.

signifier. In Saussure's linguistics, a "sound-image"—a series of sounds as they are pronounced, or a spoken word—that designate a particular "concept" or signified. While understanding the meaning of signs to be differential, Saussure's thought is still phonocentric for Derrida because it considers spoken language to be the proper object of study for linguistics, allowing an access to truths about language that writing can obscure.

signified. In Saussure's linguistics, the concept that is designated by a particular "sound-image" or spoken word. Commonly misunderstood to mean a particular object in the world referred to by the concept (which is the referent, not the signified). For Saussure and Derrida, the meaning of signifieds in the system of a given language is differential: they cannot be defined by themselves, but rely on the meanings of other signifieds in the system. Every signified can become a signifier for other signifieds. See also *sign, signifier*.

text. A term used by Derrida in phrases such as "there is nothing outside the text" to mean more than written language or books. It means any structure (linguistic, economic, historical, etc.) in which values or meanings circulate and are exchanged. Anything that we experience is always already text because it cannot enter our experience as utterly singular, isolated, and absolutely "other," but must always already have been brought within the web and circulation of meanings in terms of which we make sense of the world.

topos ouranios. A term used by Plato to designate the transcendent "heavenly place" where we can find the "Forms" that give meaning to particular objects, concepts, and entities in the world. For Derrida, there is no such place. See also *transcendental signified*.

trace. Like *différance*, *trace* refers to a condition of being and meaning that, for Derrida, is prior to the opposition between presence and absence. A trace of something is neither the full presence of that thing nor its utter absence. In *OG*, Derrida argues that every linguistic sign receives its meaning, and its status as sign, from the traces of other signs from which it can never purify itself. It is one of Derrida's terms for describing a mode of being that is in contrast to the metaphysics of presence.

transcendence/immanence. For John Frame, Western philosophy (primarily Neoplatonic philosophy) differs from the biblical account in its understanding of what it means for God to be "transcendent" and/or "immanent." For Neoplatonism, "transcendence" means that God is absolutely other and unknowable, and "immanence" means that God is indistinguishable from the world. Understood within a biblical framework, transcendence refers to God's covenant headship, and immanence refers to his covenant solidarity. There is therefore no conflict between the two terms, when understood biblically.

transcendental signified. The Western metaphysics of presence only works if it assumes that there is one concept that does not rely on any other concepts for its meaning, but can stand as the self-identical origin of all meaning. Such a concept would be a transcendental signified, transcendental because it needs to be assumed in order to guarantee the stable meaning of all signs whatever. The Western notion of God would be such a transcendental signified. Without assuming a transcendental signified, there is no self-sufficient origin and foundation for the meaningfulness of language. See also *logocentrism, metaphysics of presence.*

undecidability. In Derrida's ethics and politics, a decision is undecidable if it is impossible to have sufficient information or context to be sure that one's judgment is just. Undecidability is one of the three aporias that Derrida discusses in "Force of Law." See also *aporia*. Undecidability is what distinguishes the decision proper from mere automated rule-following. The opposite of undecidability is not indecisiveness but exhaustive calculability.

Van Til, Cornelius (1895-1987). Dutch Reformed theologian who taught at Princeton Seminary and then at Westminster Theological Seminary. Van Til's name is associated with "presuppositional" apologetics, though it is a term he did not favor. His approach is transcendental: he interrogates on what basis nonbiblical thought can make its claims about truth, meaning, and goodness. He insists that the biblical witness must be argued for as an indivisible whole and not piecemeal. See also *absolute-personality theism, equal ultimacy.*

SELECT BIBLIOGRAPHY
AND REFERENCES

For anyone seeking to come to terms with Derrida's thinking, it is imperative to read at least some of his writing firsthand. There are at least two important reasons why this is the case. The first is that, although his writing style can be described, explained, and justified, to do so is like describing a piece of music: it is much better and much quicker just to listen to it. Derrida's way of writing is part of what we might call his sensibility or his ethos, the way in which his thought holds itself in relation to its objects. Like listening to the tone of someone's voice as they lecture or watching how they hold their body, becoming familiar with the rhythms and cadences of Derrida's style can help a lot in understanding him. The second reason why it is important to read Derrida himself is that the care and circumspection with which he writes are often ignored or betrayed by those who comment on his work. Far too much criticism of Derrida is self-righteous and self-satisfied, and all in the name of attacking those who are self-righteous and self-satisfied. It is an accusation much harder to level against Derrida himself, but you would not suspect so from reading some of his critics.

In the list below, I have added comments on some of the main primary and secondary texts that I consider particularly useful for those new to Derrida's thought.

Works by Derrida, Including Interviews

Caputo, John D., ed. *Deconstruction in a Nutshell: A Conversation with Jacques Derrida*. New York: Fordham University Press, 1997. A helpful transcription of a roundtable conversation with Derrida held at Villanova in 1994 and chaired by John D. Caputo. Derrida discusses some of his ideas in an idiom that is a little easier to understand than some of his writing. A good place to start discovering Derrida for those unaccustomed to chewing through complex philosophical texts.

Derrida, Jacques. *Acts of Literature*. Edited by Derek Attridge. New York: Routledge, 1992.

———. *Acts of Religion*. Edited by Gil Anidjar. New York: Routledge, 2002.

———. "Circumfession." In *Jacques Derrida*, by Geoffrey Bennington and Jacques Derrida, 3–315. Translated by Geoffrey Bennington. Chicago: University of Chicago Press, 1993. An intimate, auto-biographical text, rich in religious themes, in which Derrida discusses his own life in a way that weaves his story in and out of themes from Augustine's *Confessions*. Derrida shows the complexity of memory (some of his recollections do not agree with each other), and the relation between self-narration and self-justification.

———. "Declarations of Independence." *New Political Science* 7, 1 (1986): 7–15.

———. "Following Theory." In *Life.After.Theory*, edited by Michael Payne and John Schad, 1–51. London: Continuum, 2003.

———. "Force of Law: The 'Mystical Foundations of Authority.'"

Translated by Mary Quaintance. In *Acts of Religion*, edited by Gil Anikjar, 230–98 (New York: Routledge, 2002). The first part of this text, entitled "From the Right to Justice" ("Du droit à la justice"), is an important text for Derrida's ethical and political thought. It discusses the difference between law and justice, the aporia of the decision, and the motif of "if there is such a thing."

———. *The Gift of Death*. Translated by David Wills. 1999; published with *Literature in Secret*; Chicago: University of Chicago Press, 2008. Contains Derrida's reading of Kierkegaard's discussion of Abraham on Mount Moriah in Genesis 22. After Kierkegaard, Derrida insists that Abraham's obedience to the immediate demand of the absolute other (i.e., God) cannot be brought within Abraham's moral code. Introduces the phrase "every other is wholly other."

———. *Given Time: I. Counterfeit Money*. Translated by Peggy Kamuf. Chicago: University of Chicago Press, 1992. A meditation on the relation between time and giving in a number of authors, leading Derrida to the conclusion that the pure gift (the gift without any reciprocal return) is impossible. All giving is co-opted into an economy of exchange, even by virtue of being recognized as a gift by the giver, in which case her self-congratulation at having given is already an economy of exchange. Also discusses the possibility and impossibility of forgiveness.

———. "Hospitality, Justice and Responsibility: A Dialogue with Jacques Derrida." In *Questioning Ethics: Contemporary Debates in Philosophy*, edited by Mark Dooley and Richard Kearney, 65–83. New York: Routledge, 1999.

———. "Letter to a Japanese Friend (Prof. Izutsu)." In *Derrida and Différance*, edited by David Wood and Robert Bernasconi, 1–5. Warwick: Parousia Press, 1985.

———. *Limited Inc*. Translated by Alan Bass and Samuel Weber. Evanston, IL: Northwestern University Press, 1988.

———. *Margins of Philosophy*. Translated by Alan Bass. Chicago: University of Chicago Press, 1982.

———. "Marx and Sons." Translated by Kelly Barry. In *Ghostly*

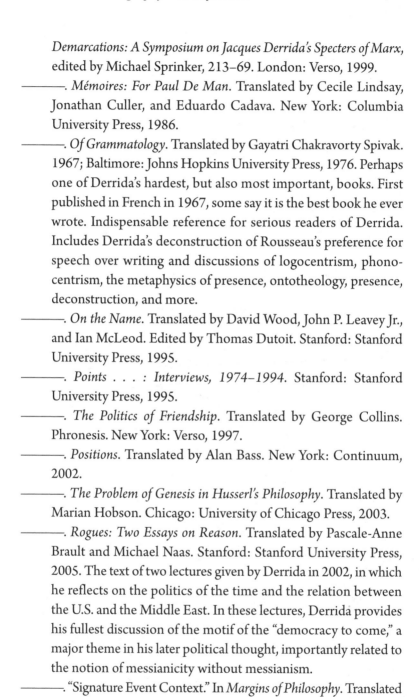

Demarcations: A Symposium on Jacques Derrida's Specters of Marx, edited by Michael Sprinker, 213–69. London: Verso, 1999.

———. *Mémoires: For Paul De Man.* Translated by Cecile Lindsay, Jonathan Culler, and Eduardo Cadava. New York: Columbia University Press, 1986.

———. *Of Grammatology.* Translated by Gayatri Chakravorty Spivak. 1967; Baltimore: Johns Hopkins University Press, 1976. Perhaps one of Derrida's hardest, but also most important, books. First published in French in 1967, some say it is the best book he ever wrote. Indispensable reference for serious readers of Derrida. Includes Derrida's deconstruction of Rousseau's preference for speech over writing and discussions of logocentrism, phono-centrism, the metaphysics of presence, ontotheology, presence, deconstruction, and more.

———. *On the Name.* Translated by David Wood, John P. Leavey Jr., and Ian McLeod. Edited by Thomas Dutoit. Stanford: Stanford University Press, 1995.

———. *Points . . . : Interviews, 1974–1994.* Stanford: Stanford University Press, 1995.

———. *The Politics of Friendship.* Translated by George Collins. Phronesis. New York: Verso, 1997.

———. *Positions.* Translated by Alan Bass. New York: Continuum, 2002.

———. *The Problem of Genesis in Husserl's Philosophy.* Translated by Marian Hobson. Chicago: University of Chicago Press, 2003.

———. *Rogues: Two Essays on Reason.* Translated by Pascale-Anne Brault and Michael Naas. Stanford: Stanford University Press, 2005. The text of two lectures given by Derrida in 2002, in which he reflects on the politics of the time and the relation between the U.S. and the Middle East. In these lectures, Derrida provides his fullest discussion of the motif of the "democracy to come," a major theme in his later political thought, importantly related to the notion of messianicity without messianism.

———. "Signature Event Context." In *Margins of Philosophy.* Translated by Alan Bass. Chicago: University of Chicago Press, 1982. The

1977 translation by Samuel Weber and Jeffrey Mehlman is used in *Limited Inc* (Evanston, IL: Northwestern University Press, 1988). A seminal essay in the development of Derrida's thought, SEC (as it is often known) explores the tensions and blind spots in the speech act theory of J. L. Austin, showing that it is not always possible to determine—as Austin tries to do—the context of a particular utterance. The essay forms part of Derrida's exchange with philosopher John Searle.

————. *Signéponge-Signsponge.* Translated by Richard Rand. New York: Columbia University Press, 1984.

————. *Speech and Phenomena, and Other Essays on Husserl's Theory of Signs.* Translated by David B. Allison. Evanston, IL: Northwestern University Press, 1973.

————. "Structure, Sign and Play in the Discourse of the Human Sciences." In *Writing and Difference.* Translated by Alan Bass. London: Routledge and Kegan Paul, 1978. Perhaps the most important essay-length piece from Derrida's earlier work, this deconstructs the structuralism that was the intellectual fashion in the Paris of his student days. The essay performs many of the same moves as we find in Derrida's readings of Rousseau and Saussure in *OG.*

————. " 'This Strange Institution Called Literature': An Interview with Jacques Derrida." In *Acts of Literature,* edited by Derek Attridge, 53–75. New York: Routledge, 1992.

————. "The Time Is out of Joint." *Diacritics* 25, 2 (1995): 85–96.

————. "The Time of a Thesis: Punctuations." In *Philosophy in France Today,* edited by Alan Montefiore, 34–50. Cambridge: Cambridge University Press, 1983.

————. *Writing and Difference.* Translated by Alan Bass. Chicago: University of Chicago Press, 1978.

Derrida, Jacques, and Maurizio Ferraris. *A Taste for the Secret.* Translated by Giacomo Donis. Malden, MA: Polity, 2001.

Derrida, Jacques, and Richard Kearney. *Debates in Continental Philosophy: Conversations with Contemporary Thinkers.* New York: Fordham University Press, 2004.

Derrida, Jacques, and Elisabeth Roudinesco. *For What Tomorrow: A Dialogue.* Translated by Jeff Fort. Stanford: Stanford University Press, 2004.

Other References

Bahnsen, Greg L. *Van Til's Apologetic: Readings and Analysis.* Philipsburg, NJ: P&R Publishing, 1988.

Beardsworth, Richard. *Derrida and the Political.* London: Routledge, 1996. A sinuous, concise, and very helpful introduction to Derrida's political thought. Not the easiest read, but very insightful.

Benson, Bruce Ellis. *Graven Ideologies: Nietzsche, Derrida and Marion on Modern Idolatry.* Downers Grove, IL: InterVarsity Press, 2002. A good example of an evangelical use of Derrida's thought to illuminate the subtleties of contemporary ideology. Broadly sympathetic to deconstruction, but raises reservations.

Calvin, Jean. *Institutes of the Christian Religion.* Translated by Henry Beveridge. Peabody, MA: Hendrickson Publishers, 2008.

Caputo, John D. *The Prayers and Tears of Jacques Derrida: Religion without Religion.* Bloomington: Indiana University Press, 1997. The best example of a theological reading of Derrida's work from a point of view very sympathetic to his thought.

Critchley, Simon. *The Ethics of Deconstruction: Derrida and Levinas.* 3rd ed. Edinburgh: Edinburgh University Press, 2014. Seminal book in making the argument that deconstruction has an ethics and a politics. Still one of the finest and most sensitive readings of Derrida's ethics, particularly in relation to the influential thought of Emmanuel Levinas.

Culler, Jonathan. *On Deconstruction: Theory and Criticism after Structuralism.* Ithaca, NY: Cornell University Press, 2007.

Edwards, Jonathan. *The "Miscellanies."* The Works of Jonathan Edwards, edited by Thomas Schafer, vol. 13. New Haven: Yale University Press, 1994.

Frame, John M. *Apologetics to the Glory of God: An Introduction.* Phillipsburg, NJ: P&R Publishing, 1994.

―――. *Cornelius Van Til: An Analysis of His Thought.* Phillipsburg, NJ: P&R Publishing, 1995.

―――. *The Doctrine of God.* Phillipsburg, NJ: P&R Publishing, 2002.

―――. *The Doctrine of the Christian Life.* Phillipsburg, NJ: P&R Publishing, 2008.

―――. *The Doctrine of the Knowledge of God.* Phillipsburg, NJ: P&R Publishing, 1987.

―――. *A History of Western Philosophy and Theology.* Phillipsburg, NJ: P&R Publishing, 2015.

Hägglund, Martin. *Radical Atheism: Derrida and the Time of Life.* Stanford: Stanford University Press, 2008.

Hale, Jacob Gabriel. "Derrida, Van Til and the Metaphysics of Postmodernism." *Reformed Perspectives Magazine* 6, 19 (2004), http://reformedperspectives.org/ (accessed January 2016).

Heidegger, Martin. *Identity and Difference.* Translated by J. Stambaugh. New York: Harper & Row, 1969.

Hill, Leslie. *The Cambridge Introduction to Jacques Derrida.* Cambridge: Cambridge University Press, 2007. One of the best one-volume introductions to Derrida. A deeply researched and well-written book that focuses on Derrida's engagement with literature. Hill explains Derrida's thought precisely and carefully.

Malabou, Catherine. *La chambre du milieu: De Hegel aux neurosciences.* Paris: Éditions Hermann, 2009.

McGrath, Alastair E. *Christian Theology: An Introduction.* 2nd ed. Oxford: Basil Blackwell, 1995.

Newbigin, Lesslie. *Foolishness to the Greeks: The Gospel and Western Culture.* Grand Rapids: Eerdmans, 1986.

Nietzsche, Friedrich. *The Anti-Christ, Ecce Homo, Twilight of the Idols and Other Writings.* Edited by Aaron Ridley and Judith Norman. Translated by Judith Norman. Cambridge: Cambridge University Pres, 2005.

―――. *Philosophy and Truth: Selections from Nietzsche's Notebooks of the Early 1870s.* Edited by Daniel Breazeale. Atlantic Highlands, NJ: Humanities Press, 1970.

Peeters, Benoît. *Derrida: A Biography.* Translated by Andrew Brown. Cambridge: Polity Press, 2012. The most authoritative, comprehensive biography of Derrida. Helpful for situating his different books in the context of his own life and times.

Pickstock, Catherine. *After Writing: On the Liturgical Consummation of Philosophy.* Oxford: Blackwell, 1997.

Raschke, Carl. *The Next Reformation: Why Evangelicals Must Embrace Postmodernity.* Grand Rapids: Baker Academic, 2004.

Shakespeare, Steven. *Derrida and Theology.* London: T & T Clark, 2009. To my mind, the best general or "impartial" introduction to Derrida's engagement with theological motifs. Includes a helpful chapter summarizing readers of Derrida's theology, both positive and negative, including their critiques of his thought.

Smith, James K. A. *Jacques Derrida: Live Theory.* New York: Continuum, 2005. A helpful, book-length treatment of Derrida to sit alongside Smith's briefer engagement in *Who's Afraid of Postmodernism?* Not writing from an overtly Christian point of view, Smith seeks to defend Derrida from his detractors as he combats what he calls the "Derrida-monster" and the "Derrida myth."

———. *Who's Afraid of Postmodernism? Taking Derrida, Lyotard, and Foucault to Church.* Grand Rapids: Baker Academic, 2006. A short, introductory text dealing with Foucault and Lyotard as well as Derrida. Smith seeks to show how these postmodern thinkers echo biblical concerns, while he attempts to rescue them from a series of misunderstandings.

Van Til, Cornelius. *Christian Apologetics.* Phillipsburg, NJ: P&R Publishing, 2003.

———. *Christian Theistic Ethics.* Philipsburg, NJ: Presbyterian & Reformed, 1974.

———. *The Defense of the Faith.* 4th ed. Edited by K. Scott Oliphint. Phillipsburg, NJ: P&R Publishing, 2008.

———. *The Intellectual Challenge of the Gospel.* Phillipsburg, NJ: P&R Publishing, 1953.

————. *An Introduction to Systematic Theology*. Phillipsburg, NJ: Presbyterian and Reformed, 1979.

Volf, Miroslav. *Exclusion and Embrace: A Theological Exploration of Identity, Otherness, and Reconciliation*. Nashville: Abingdon Press, 1996.

Ward, Graham. *Barth, Derrida and the Language of Theology*. Cambridge: Cambridge University Press, 1995.

Warfield, Benjamin B. *The Inspiration and Authority of the Bible*. Philadelphia: Presbyterian and Reformed, 1967.

Wilson, Douglas. "Pretending to Leave Modernity Behind." Review of *Who's Afraid of Postmodernism?* by James K. A. Smith. Doug wils.com/books/pretending-to-leave-modernity-behind.html (accessed January 2016).

INDEX OF SCRIPTURE

INDEX OF SUBJECTS AND NAMES

Christopher Watkin (MPhil, PhD, Jesus College, Cambridge) researches and writes on modern and contemporary French thought, atheism, and religion. He works as senior lecturer in French studies at Monash University in Melbourne, Australia, where he lives with his wife, Alison, and son, Benjamin. His recent books include *French Philosophy Today: New Figures of the Human in Badiou, Meillassoux, Malabou, Serres and Latour* (2016), *Difficult Atheism: Post-Theological Thinking in Badiou, Meillassoux and Nancy* (2011), and *From Plato to Postmodernism: The Story of Western Culture through Philosophy, Literature and Art* (2011). He is also the author of *Jacques Derrida* (2017) in the P&R Great Thinkers series.

He blogs on French philosophy and the academic life at christopher watkin.com and is a cofounder of audialterampartem.com, a site with the twin aims of bringing evangelical and Reformed theology into deep conversation with modern French philosophy and of encouraging scholars and scholarship working at the nexus of those traditions. You can find him on Twitter @DrChrisWatkin.